California Public Works Projects

California Public Works Projects

MANAGING CONTRACTS & RESOLVING DISPUTES

1999-2000 Edition

By Ernest C. Brown, Esq., P.E.
Member of the California Bar
Licensed Civil Engineer
San Francisco & Newport Beach, California

Publishers Design Group
Santa Rosa, California

Library of Congress Card Number: 99-65953

ISBN: 1-929170-00-9

Printed September, 1999

Book and cover design by Robert Brekke
Summary Editing by Kimberly Mercier

Ernest Brown & Company
www.ernestbrown.com

Published by
Publishers Design Group
Santa Rosa, CA 95402
www.publishersdesign.com

Printed in U.S.A.

CONTENTS

Photography Credits

Cover photograph: Courtesy of The Bancroft Library, University of California, Berkeley. From the collection titled *Construction Photographs of the Golden Gate Bridge.*

Pages 1, 19, 33, 67, 75, 85, 105, 141, and 147. Historic California Courthouse photos. Courtesy of the Department of Special Collections, University of California Library, Davis California.

Page 131. Los Angeles County Courthouse. Photo courtesy of the Los Angeles Superior Court.

Page 119. California State Court of Appeals, 4th Appellate District, Division 2, Riverside, California. Courtesy of Swinerton & Walberg and A C Martin Partners, Inc. Architects/Engineers: A C Martin Partners, Inc.; Construction: Swinerton & Walberg; Photography: LENOIR Photography.

Pages 13, 53, 111, 125, and 151. Courtesy of Publishers Design Group. Photography: Robert Brekke.

I would like to express my appreciation to my wife, Suzanne Greischel Brown, a San Francisco Architect, for her enthusiasm and fresh viewpoints on this project.

Foreword

Constructors, their employees and vendors, enjoy the challenge of building projects. Yet, a book on public works construction law would rarely be their focus for an enjoyable afternoon of summer reading. Not withstanding this statement, it is a pleasure to write the Foreword for a primer on that subject. Ernie Brown, Esq., PE, the author, is one of the industry's most active construction lawyers, teachers, and contributors to the AGC's Legal Advisory Committee. It is an undeniable fact that knowing the rules of law that govern public works construction projects within California is an essential element of every construction professional's education. Knowledge of California's public works laws is critical to ensure the state agencies and, in turn the public, are obtaining the best construction project for the dollar. Further, the contractor is afforded the protection of specific contractual rights and a fair and level playing field for achieving a high degree of quality, timely performance, and profitability.

In California, public agencies turn to the construction industry to build projects of enormous importance and scope. Schools, hospitals, roadways, and bridges would not exist without this public-private partnership of government agencies and the engineering and construction industry. The Associated General Contractors of California has worked long and hard with the State of California, the League of Cities, and many other governmental agencies across the state to improve and perfect that partnership. It is with great pride that our association has worked with attorneys and elected public officials in the improvement and clarification of these laws, as well as the promotion of fairness and business judgment in the government contracting that is conducted in the State. Again, books of this kind further those ends by educating us all on the important, "rules of the road" for public works projects.

Thomas Holtzman
Executive Vice President
Associated General Contractors Of California
Sacramento, California

June, 1999

Introduction

The purpose of this manual is to help contractors, owners, architects, public agencies and engineers understand California construction contract law, fulfill their legal responsibilities, avoid typical project difficulties and disputes, as well as recognize when they need the assistance of specialized legal counsel. It is an updated and expanded version of the author's 1995 *Public Works; Contracts and Litigation*, published by the California Continuing Education of the Bar (CEB - May 1995).

California businesses and public agencies expend vast sums for construction and design services. The private construction market in California is nearly $20 billion per year, including housing. More than 7,000 public agencies within the state of California generate over $10 billion per year in public works construction. Despite the size of this market and the importance of public facilities, California private and public works law is complex and often misunderstood. Many project disputes arise as a result.

This manual covers the most important California statutes affecting public projects, as well as key California court decisions. It also offers practical suggestions for well-managed projects.

Running through this book is an assumption that the reader has a basic knowledge of the construction industry and familiarity with contract law. However, to help the greatest possible number of people, the legal language used in describing the ruling court decisions has been somewhat simplified — and therefore generalized. The case examples given are for illustrative purposes only. Furthermore, there are constant changes in the public works statutes and interpretative cases are issued weekly.

As such, readers should not assume that a court's decision in a particular case will apply in all similar cases, as the laws are complex and every court decision is based on numerous factors. Nor should the reader assume that every statute cited remains unchanged. In addition, the role of attorneys specializing in construction law includes both active help for contractors and state agencies. Clear agreements prevent disputes from occurring (by ensuring clear and proper language in public works contracts before the parties sign) and help resolve claims issues if they arise.

This manual provides practical information and answers the typical questions asked within public agencies and construction industry participants. However, because each public works project is unique and each contract contains specific requirements, the advice of legal counsel is strongly recommended for all parties entering any contract for a state or local public works construction project. This manual only briefly mentions legal aspects of federal construction projects, a subject covered by numerous other handbooks and manuals.

Many misunderstandings and disputes, as well as costly litigation, can be avoided with careful planning. This manual provides an overview of the most important steps that should be taken by the parties before entering into a contract for a public works project, red flags of problem situations that will require immediate attention, and a guide to those steps that have been proven to be of assistance in resolving those problems when they arise.

This manual contains statutes and cases updated through April 30, 1999.

IMPORTANT

This Handbook is a general guide to California public works law. It should not be relied upon for legal guidance or advice. The summaries of cases and legal principles contained in these materials are appropriate for management training and education, not as a substitute for a professional legal opinion based upon the facts and an in-depth review of applicable statutes and case law.

Chapter 1

THE CALIFORNIA MARKET AND PROJECT DELIVERY SYSTEMS

The Old Woodland Courthouse
Courtesy University of California Library, Davis California

Summary:
The opening chapter briefly discusses the California market, as well as the standard construction delivery systems utilized in California. The various professionals and business entities involved in projects are described, in addition to their typical interrelationships and ingrained sources of conflict. Partnering and team building consisting of the owner, designer and construction professionals are discussed along with the possible pitfalls that may be encountered. The importance of the construction manager and his (or her) role is also reviewed. Project organization options, as well as various methods of execution of a project, are discussed in some detail.

§ 1.1 CALIFORNIA CONSTRUCTION MARKET

This **manual** presents an overview of the **California construction market** and summarizes some of the most important laws that have been promulgated to regulate the market.

Construction represents a critical and growing segment of the state's economy. In 1999, the California construction market will generate nearly $20 billion in private construction, including homebuilding. In addition, public works construction of $10 billion will account for a large portion of the annual budgets of many local public agencies, particularly water districts, sanitary districts, bridge and highway districts, schools, cities, and counties.

The California **private market** has been propelled by a strong homebuilding market, rapidly escalating commercial rents in San Francisco, rapid growth in the Silicon Valley and Southern California, and investment in modern facilities for the high technology, entertainment and aerospace sectors. The only sector of the California economy that has seen reduced revenues from the past decade is the defense industry. Even in that sector, military base reuse initiatives, including Economic Benefit Conveyances to local communities of former base properties, have provided many diverse opportunities for significant construction projects.

The California **public market** has responded to the state's increasing population and business strength. Following the bankruptcy of the county of Orange in 1994, the credit ratings of California public agencies have recovered. Public bonds for toll roads and airports are highly innovative and are highly attractive to long term investors. These represent billions of locally raised taxes such as state income tax, county property taxes, use taxes, gas taxes, special district assessments, and public bonds. In addition, these funds are often supplemented with federal grants, especially for airports, water treatment, and roadways.

In summary, the California market is strong and offers a stark contrast to the near depression levels of the early 1990s, when construction cranes were nearly an endangered species in the state.

For lawyers and construction professionals, the challenges have shifted from serious collection problems with private and public entities,

2

weekly trips to bankruptcy court, and company liquidations of less than ten years ago. Instead, substantial opportunities for growth and profit exist for those firms that can flexibly adapt to client opportunities.

§ 1.2 PROJECT DELIVERY APPROACHES

"Project delivery" refers to the manner in which a project is accomplished from design through construction. This section presents an overview of the common project delivery approaches used for public works projects.

§ 1.2.1 *What is the Project?*

What does the owner want? A simple question, perhaps, but one rarely asked at the beginning of the project. Several very basic questions must be asked by the project team early in the process. The owner is the most cost-conscious, the architect most interested in the "look and feel," the contractor concerned with "buildability," and the ultimate user is focused on the practicality and cost of maintenance. All see different issues when contemplating a major project.

During the early planning stages, the essential **project goals** and objectives must be **identified and prioritized**. Speed in delivery, ease of operation, dramatic design elements, innovation, national expertise, local content, proven technology, and cost efficiency can rarely be reached simultaneously. Choices must be made at a high level of the client organization at a very early stage. In a sense, this effort is a creative way of defining success on the project.

What will be the shape of the managerial and administrative groups that will organize and manage the design and the construction processes? Most owner organizations do not have a sufficient depth of design and construction expertise to self-build their own projects.

What is the risk profile of the project? Beware the owner that is building a one of a kind, once in a generation facility. Airports, local jails, sewage treatment facilities, churches, and retirement communities are typical examples. The nature of the risks should drive the organizational structure employed by the owner.

On the other hand, repetitive projects for experienced and well financed owners, such as stores for Wal Mart, storage tanks for Exxon, cargo facilities for the major railroads, roadways and bridges for Cal Trans, and hangAr projects for Boeing are examples of projects that should, generally, go right. But these also have risks, although less obvious. They can be catastrophic if not properly addressed. Generally, many low frequency, high severity risks can be covered by extensive insurance policies. But organizational structure can substantially affect the risk and the availability of certain types of insurance.

§ 1.2.2 *Project Organization Options*

The major project organizational options available to the owner are: a) Design-Bid-Build; b) Project Management/CM; c) Design-Build; and d) Multiple Prime. In addition, the execution of the project may be accomplished by e) Fast Track; f) Turnkey Projects; g) Performance Based Contracting; h) Design-Build-Own-Transfer (BOT); and the use of i) Partnering and Team Building.

§ 1.2.2(a) *Design-Bid-Construct*

The traditional approach has been to separately engage design and construction firms. In this approach, an architect or engineer completes the design prior to an owner soliciting a general contractor to construct the project. Next, the owner provides interested general contractors with plans and specifications. A general contractor is then selected, and construction begins[1].

§ 1.2.2(b) *Project Management*

Since most owners do not have sufficient staff or expertise for the peak period of project design and construction, they generally will retain a project management firm for projects of more than $50 million.

Project managers are generally administratively oriented, serving as an extension of the owner's staff. The key expertise of retained construction management or project management firms should be management, not construction or design. In fact, in public construction, the independent CM or PM will generally refrain from direct design or construction duties. Instead, it will develop the selection process for designers, cost estimating and testing firms, perform extensive reviews of their expertise, develop and administer their contracts, provide expertise on constructability, manage relationships with funding and oversight agencies, and provide a system of communications, public information, emergency response, and policy advice for the owner.

An example is major airport work, where CM/PM firms manage infrastructure from conceptual studies of aviation alternatives through the design and construction process, the start-up and warranty work, and into the next cycle of conceptual design, at all times working to keep the public entity and elected representatives informed and able to make key decisions.

§ 1.2.2(c) The Design-Build Process

The Design-Build process employs a single entity providing both design and construction services, so a single entity remains responsible for all aspects of a project. Typically, a design-build oriented, general contractor provides the design and construction services. However, an architectural firm may provide the design services and hire a general contractor on a consulting basis for the construction phase; and, in this case, the architectural firm will be held responsible for all aspects of the project[2].

The design-build process places sole responsibility for a project on one entity that provides all design and construction services. Typically, a general contractor or construction company is the single entity and employs architects or engineers (directly or on a consulting basis) for the design phase. The construction company itself then performs the construction phase of the project. The design-build methodology provides savings in cost and time because the entire project is managed and constructed by a single entity, thereby eliminating the difficulties of dealing with multiple entities on one project.

The design-build approach is seldom used by general law public agencies because of competitive bidding requirements. Charter public agencies may utilize this approach if their charters so provide. In addition, the Contract Code allows great flexibility when a public project is privately financed, at least in part.

§ 1.2.2(d) Multiple Prime Contracting

This method of contracting assumes the owner can manage multiple prime contractors on a jobsite, the role of the typical general contractor responsibility. Unfortunately, this means there is no single bidder with cost and schedule responsibility. The CM/PM hired to perform such a multiple prime project will often argue that they should have no responsibility for overall budget or schedule of the project. This leaves the owner in the position of absorbing the majority of the risk for cost and schedule overruns.

§ 1.2.2(e) Fast Track Projects

In **fast-track**, or phased design and construction, schedule advantages are achieved in time critical projects by allowing construction to begin before the final drawings are completed for a project in which "time is of the essence" to the owner. The project is constructed utilizing preliminary plans and specifications, and is thereafter modified as necessary without price increases.[3] Unfortunately, this means there is no fixed price or firm schedule for the overall project at the outset. As the design of the project is being put into concrete before the design is complete, there are few opportunities to fine-tune the design to maximize cost savings. Civil excavations, pier work, and caissons may be undersized or oversized, since the final structural design may not be complete. This method promotes schedule savings, but runs the risk of dramatic cost overruns.

§ 1.2.2(f) Turnkey Projects

The turnkey project involves an owner contracting to buy a completed project from a contractor, who is essentially the developer of the property on which the project is constructed. The owner has virtually no control over the day to day aspects of the project. The courts state that a turnkey project is "a project in which all the owner need do is 'turn the key' in the lock to open the building, with nothing remaining to be done and all risks to be assumed by the contractor."

§ 1.2.2(g) Performance Based Contracting

In this approach, the owner sets criteria, from a number of square feet of warehouse space to the output of an electrical or steam co-generation plant, and leaves the design and construction of the facility pretty much to the design build contractor or industrial vendor. Again, the looser the criteria, the greater the chance the owner's and contractor's vision of a successful result will differ. Can you guess which vision will cost less money?

§ 1.2.2(h) Design-Build-Operate-Transfer

With the long delivery times associated with public projects, there is a trend toward the public entity leasing facilities with an end of term buy out.

This has been actively pursued by wastewater treatment firms who have design, construction management, and plant operations expertise. By applying unparalleled expertise, worldwide buying power (from computer systems to chemicals), access to capital (certain engineering firm's creditworthiness exceeds many public entities) and a huge worldwide staffing depth, such firms can offer dramatic cost savings to local public entities who are strapped for cash or bonding capacity.

Many local agencies and labor unions see such DBOT arrangements as passing control and decision making authority to a private entity in contravention to the public trust.

However, the public generally wants clean water more than burgeoning public entities, so the trend appears on the upswing.

§ 1.2.2(i) Partnering and Team Building

The role played by partnering and team building has passed from fad to established practice. Much like a management retreat in a large company, these meetings build understanding and trust between the owner, designer and construction professionals. While knowing more about one's counterparts in the public agency may not prevent a major conflict later, it can build sufficient trust that can make many of the little decisions and problems on jobs easier to resolve.

Team building can be taken too far. It is probably fine to have a company wide picnic, but it may be illegal to take a boating trip with the project inspector, especially if you are the contractor, and you bought him the boat!

In fact, there has been a limited backlash against partnering. There are certain, very vocal parties that claim they were burned in the partnering process. In one case, the contractor explained that his losses should be shared by the owner since they were "partnering" under the agreement. The Uniform Partnership Act defines "partners" as two or more persons or entities doing business for profit. And, partners have fiduciary duties of disclosure and good faith. As such, the "team building" term is often used by owners and contractors and their lawyers, who understand that partnering can be a loaded word in the courtroom.

§ 1.3 PROJECT ENTITIES AND RELATIONSHIPS

There are a wide variety of parties that participate in a large construction project. Since projects are built by people, their legal relationships often control the success of the project. While this is an exceedingly boring topic for most industry professionals, these issues are the foundation of construction project law.

§ 1.3.1 Defining the Project Parties

It is important to recognize the legal relationships of the parties in construction projects, even though it runs the risk of burdening the reader with the customary legalese. For the design of a project, the **owner** generally contracts with independent design professionals for

7

the construction of a specific project or contracts to buy a completed project from a contractor/developer. An **architect** is defined as one who is licensed to practice architecture in the state of California.[4]

A person who offers or performs "professional services which require the skills of an architect in the planning of sites, and the design, in whole or in part, of buildings, or groups of buildings and structures" is engaging in the practice of architecture.[5]

An **engineer** is one who possesses education, training, and experience in engineering services and has special knowledge in various areas, including design of public or private utilities.[6] The three primary areas of specialty within the engineering sciences are civil engineering,[7] electrical engineering, and mechanical engineering.[8] An engineer is usually retained by the architect as an independent contractor and is responsible for detailed calculations, drawings, and specification preparation.

A **general contractor** is an entity (individual, corporation, partnership, etc.) that constructs, alters, repairs, improves, moves, or demolishes any building, highway, or other structure.[9] This definition applies to both subcontractors and specialty contractors.[10]

A **construction manager**[11] is typically described as one who acts as a construction overseer, managing the day-to-day on-site activities of the entire project. The construction manager generally does not perform actual construction services or provide any work with his or her own forces. The construction manager acts in the capacity of an agent of the owner and receives fees as his or her sole compensation. He or she negotiates contracts with the various contractors, schedules and coordinates their work so it will be in accordance with the project plans and specifications, and oversees cost management. In California, there is no strict requirement for a construction manager[12] to be licensed as either a contractor or an architect.

§ 1.3.2 _Organizational Relationships_

§ 1.3.2(a) _The Design Relationship (Architect or Engineer)_

The relationship between the owner and the design professional is established by contract and by case law. While the subject of malpractice is a course in and of itself (the author has participated in such courses in the past), the principal relationships that will occur during the course of the project among the architect, engineer, owner and contractor are established in the initial design agreement.

By far, the most widely utilized and accepted standard contract between an owner and the design professional is the American Institute of Architects, (AIA) document B141. This standard form was specifically designed to address the owner-architect relationship. It contains many provisions that specify the duties and responsibilities of the design professional and the owner, and forms the basis of almost all contracts between owners and architects for residential and commercial building projects, as well as establishes the guidelines for the architect's consultant agreements with its engineering and other associated firms.

However, the parties may choose to execute a contract that does not utilize the AIA B141 standard form. In either situation, the contract governs the rights, duties, and responsibilities of the parties. Thus, it is important that the owner determine exactly what those responsibilities will be when drafting the contract in order to avoid future disputes.

The services a design professional performs are varied and are determined by the contract executed with the owner. Services range from designing the structure itself and estimating the total project cost to assisting in the overall bidding process, inspecting construction, issuing change orders, and giving final approval for all progress and final payments made to contractors by the public entity.

The design professional's primary responsibility is to prepare and provide plans and specifications that the contractor can use to build the project; however, responsibility does not end once the plans and specifications are complete. It continues throughout the project with the design professional interpreting and revising the plans and specifications in order to address actual construction conditions the contractor encounters in the field. The AIA B-141 outlines the primary services that the architect will perform, generally for a fixed fee, and also lists other services, which are generally compensated on an hourly basis. It is important to budget the necessary construction phase services, as well as other soft costs, such as appearances before planning commissions and related architectural support services.

The owner also has responsibilities to the design professional.[13] The most important obligation of an owner is to provide complete and accurate information regarding the design objectives of the project. This information should include budget restraints, site conditions, easement, zoning, and land use restrictions. In addition, the owner is obligated to pay the design professional for his or her services.

§ 1.3.2(b) Owner and General Contractor

Once the plans and specifications have been prepared by the design professional, the owner can solicit bids from general contractors through advertising.[14] The public entity owner then awards the contract to the lowest responsible bidder.[15]

Once the requirements of bidding and awarding the public works contract have been satisfied, the general contractor awarded the contract begins construction. Because all subcontractors are required to be listed in the general contractor's bid package submitted to the public entity, the general contractor will have already negotiated contracts with its subcontractors.[16] The responsibilities of the general contractor encompass only the construction phase of the project.[17] A standard contract form that is widely utilized by public entities contracting with general contractors is AIA document A201. This standard form, or the particular language of the contract itself, govern the responsibilities of both parties. It must be specially modified for use in California and is grossly inadequate for public works construction without substantial modification and additional statutory language.

Generally, the contractor is obligated to build the project in conformity with the plans and specifications, which means not only strictly adhering to the project design, as set forth in the plans and specifications, but also guaranteeing the materials and providing quality workmanship. In addition, the general contractor must bring to the attention of the design professional any errors or omissions in the plans and specifications, coordinate all phases of construction with its various subcontractors, and arrange for all inspections.

The public entity owner is obligated to provide complete and accurate information to the general contractor, which is the same as its responsibility to the design professional. In addition, the public agency owner is typically required to obtain all necessary permits, approvals, and payment provisions which are important to the general contractor, and are usually based on the progress of construction. Schedule parameters are also defined in the contract documents.

§ 1.3.3(c) Owner and Construction Manager

A public agency owner may decide to employ a construction manager whose role is to act as an agent of the public agency. Competitive bidding requirements do not apply to an owner-construction manager relationship; however, some agencies take the position that the contract must still be awarded to the lowest responsible bidder and adhere to all other competitive bidding requirements,[18] despite the fact that the construction manager is acting as the owner's agent.

The construction manager has several responsibilities. The primary obligations are cost management, construction scheduling, design review, bid packaging, and, of course, day-to-day project site management.

During the design phase of a public works project, a construction manager reviews conceptual designs and provides advice on construction feasibility and the selection of materials and equipment. In addition, he or she develops and updates the construction schedules, prepares the project budget and construction cost estimates, and prepares a bid analysis and award recommendations after the bidding process. Once construction begins, the construction manager is responsible for conducting on-site meetings with the various parties involved, updating the project schedule, implementing the change order system, and reviewing proposed change order requests. More importantly, he or she inspects the ongoing construction of the project, establishes and implements procedures for expediting the processing and approval of shop drawings, provides progress reports to the owner, and coordinates all work to be performed by the various subcontractors involved in the project.

Chapter 2

PROJECT RISK CHECKLIST

California State Building, San Francisco
Photo by Robert Brekke

Summary:
A simple technique for evaluating project risks is discussed in this chapter, as well as risks a company may be willing to absorb. A sample project risk checklist can be found in the Appendix. Various types of owners are reviewed, as well as projects that are most risk prone. Building types which tend to generate major claims are identified, along with their specific risks. The author points out that speculative financing of projects should be avoided. Determining the project budget and the funding source for the project is discussed, in addition to the importance of reviewing contract provisions and investigating potential project participants.

§ 2.1 EVALUATING PROJECT RISK

Construction project risk identification is based upon the known losses and failures that occur with known frequency in the industry. There are statistics kept by governmental agencies and professional liability carriers regarding construction risks and losses, and the measurement of those risks is truly a science. Equally so, the avoidance of risk and the mitigation of damage are arts.

While there are numerous methodologies for risk avoidance, a simple technique is the listing of all known project risks, the probability of their occurrence, the minimum and maximum outcomes, the expected values of those outcomes (frequency x severity), the availability and cost of insurance for the risk duration, reasonable mitigation steps, and the party most likely to be able to prevent, absorb or insure the adverse result, if it occurs.

After an overall and in-depth project evaluation, a risk management plan can be developed and implemented. It should be emphasized that safety is a moral value and must never be compromised.

During the course of certain projects, it may be appropriate to evaluate the potential profit that might be generated from certain activities versus their expenses and financial risks. Furthermore, each company may have a certain type of risk with which it is comfortable.

For example, a company may wish to design and build certain types of industrial plants, but wish to refrain from operating them due to the different set of risks and insurance programs associated with such ventures. As another example, a company may be willing to take on a design-build-operate water treatment project over thirty years, but not be willing to absorb the risk of increasing costs of chemicals, changes in environmental laws, or union labor rate changes. It may, on the other hand, be willing to take the variable interest rate risk on borrowed funds.

Obviously, any situation or risk where personal injury or death are potential outcomes raise the most serious concerns. Those concerns obviously go beyond a mere monetary analysis and encompass moral and ethical responsibilities as well.

Some risks, unfortunately, cannot be insured, or avoided. Sometimes the magnitude of those risks make it inappropriate to proceed with the project.

§ 2.2 RISK CHECKLIST

The following are general descriptions of the types of risks that should be considered in any project evaluation.

§ 2.2.1 *Ownership*

The type of owner is the most important risk factor. In general, well funded, stable, locally-oriented clients with long term relationships with the project participants are preferred risks. Homeowner associations, small government entities, non-profit organizations, school districts, churches, individuals, and community groups are the most risk prone.

§ 2.2.2 *Building Type*

There are several key building types that generate major risks.

Obviously, refineries, industrial plants, and oil and gas pipelines pose natural risks of explosion and fire. But the quality standards for such facilities are extremely high, and these type of risks are generally insurable by the owner and contractor.

Generally, any public structure is risky due to the possibility of personal injury claims by the public. Airports, sports and entertainment complexes, retail and other similar facilities generate a disproportional amount of slip and fall, public liability and related claims.

Condo associations are often pre-fabricated class actions. They are personal homes that by their nature are meant to be economical, often meaning cheaply constructed and often lacking in high quality amenities. These are the worst type of residential projects from a risk standpoint. In many California markets, participation in such projects is nearly uninsurable.

Certain projects may appear innocuous, but can be extremely risky. While the design and construction of water pipelines in the desert would appear to be a low risk venture, such a project led to a $146 million claim in Arizona. Not only was the desert environment particularly corrosive to the pipeline system, the loss of water flow to Phoenix and the threat of major flash floods was a risk the owner did not wish to accept. Loss of water or other critical needs during critical agricultural or manufacturing periods arguably could have generated untolled consequential damages.

There are other risks whenever a remote job is bid. For example, availability of materials and labor productivity in such areas as the eastern Sierras or the California deserts may be a significant risk on large jobs.

§ 2.2.3 *Financing Method*

While there is no substitute for cash in the bank, speculative financing schemes should be avoided. Where there is a significant risk that up-front investment in a project may not be repaid, the reward for participation should be substantial. While the Orange County Bankruptcy cast doubt on public entity financing, it was a rare event. Generally, public entities are able to pay the base contract amounts. It is always a good idea to determine from where the funds will be coming and the budget that the owner has set, including contingency.

§ 2.2.4 *Location of Project*

Urban, suburban, and rural projects all have their associated risks. The principal issue is whether the designer and contractor have extensive enough experience, familiarity, and professional contacts in the region to fairly evaluate and effectively mitigate the local risks.

§ 2.2.5 *Contract Provisions*

While it may be impossible to grade the rationality of project contracts on a one to ten scale, there are substantial differences in terms. The presence of lengthy disclaimer statements, indemnities, or outrageous insurance provisions may be a tip-off towards the type of contracts administration that may be expected as well.

It is critical to review every unfamiliar contract. Beware of type-written contracts that sound like the standard AIA or EJCDC forms. Often, they will contain incredibly oppressive terms. It is a better practice to use the standard forms, but use a separate addendum to set forth additions, deletions, and modifications. The form itself should reflect these additions, deletions, and modifications by way of editorial hash marks, carets, and references to the addenda.

§ 2.2.6 *How to Investigate the Parties*

The most direct methods of checking out a potential party to a contract are to check their references and discuss their business practices with those firms that are most familiar with their company.

With the advent of computer data bases, there is very little information about an individual or company that is not in the public record. Current and past litigation history, licensed discipline, bankruptcy, tax liens, credit history, and numerous other factors are available immediately over the Internet. The most important legal issue with regard to the owner is their status of ownership of the property and their financing. Both are generally available through a preliminary title search, at little or no cost.

In addition, ENR, Lexis/Nexis, and D&B services report extensively on firms and individuals in the industry.

Chapter 3

DESIGN AGREEMENTS

The Old Downieville Courthouse
Courtesy University of California Library, Davis California

Summary:

This chapter discusses the design process and criteria for selecting architects and engineers (A/Es) in the private and public sector based on Government Code Sections 4525-4529.5 ("The Little Brooks Act"). The regulations that a state agency must adhere to and the steps that must be taken by that agency in the bid and selection process are also discussed. Design Agreements are broken down into sub-parts. The key clauses that must be included in the Design Agreement and the necessary content of each clause are also covered in detail.

§ 3.1 SELECTION OF DESIGN PROFESSIONALS

There are no formal legal rules for selection of A/Es in the private sector. However, the public sector has highly developed rules. The provisions of the Contract Code dealing with contracts for services rendered to the state do not apply to contracts for architectural and engineering services that are subject to Government Code § 4525—4529.5, the "Little Brook's Act"[19] (The state of California legislation is referred to as the Little Brooks Act and is based on the Brooks Act, a U.S. federal statute which specifies qualifications-based selection of architectural and engineering services). The following discussion summarizes the key California provisions that are of particular importance in the selection of the design professional.

The selection of design professionals by a state or local agency shall be on the basis of demonstrated competence and on the professional qualifications necessary for the satisfactory performance of the services required."[20] State agencies must therefore adopt by regulation, and local agencies may adopt by ordinance, procedures to assure that design professionals are engaged on this basis and that their services are provided at fair and reasonable prices to the public agencies. In addition, the agencies must ensure the maximum participation of small business firms and must specifically prohibit unlawful practices such as rebates, kickbacks, and conflicts of interest.[21]

The regulations governing the selection of private architectural and engineering firms for the state of California projects are provided by the Department of General Services.[22] However, in negotiating a fee and executing a contract for design professional services, a state public agency must follow specified procedures outlined in the Contract Code.[23] After notice has been given to the successful design professional firm that it has selected, the state agency is required to provide written instructions to the firm that contain information regarding contract negotiations. Negotiations must begin within 14 days after the successful firm has been notified.[24]

Once the negotiations are complete, a contract must be executed within 45 days.[25] If an impasse is reached by the parties during the negotiations, the state agency may terminate the negotiations and begin negotiating with the next most qualified design professional firm.[26]

Firms are encouraged to submit statements of qualifications and performance data to the state agency on an annual basis.[27] In addition, the state agency must announce a statement of all projects requiring design professional services in publications of the respective professional societies.

The agency must evaluate current statements of qualifications it has on file along with others that may be submitted regarding the proposed project, and must conduct interviews with at least three of the qualified firms. Thereafter, the most highly qualified design professional is selected by the state agency.[28] If the selection is conducted by a local agency, that agency may follow the procedures required of state agencies, but the local public agency must enumerate the selection criteria and method of selection so as to avoid unnecessary bid protests and project delays.[29]

The public agency must negotiate a contract with the "best qualified firm... at compensation which the state agency head determines is fair and reasonable to the state of California or the political subdivision involved."[30] If there are more than three successive negotiations with firms that do not result in a contract, then the state agency must select additional qualified firms and repeat the procedures.[31] When the selection conducted is by a local agency, the agency may follow the procedures required of state agencies.[32]

The provisions discussed above do not apply where the state or local agency determines that the services needed are of a more technical nature and involve little professional judgment and that issuing a request for bids (rather than statements of qualifications) would be in the public interest.[33]

In general, the procedures for selecting construction managers follow the rules for designers. Firms proposing to provide construction project management services must provide evidence that the individual or firm, and its personnel carrying out on-site responsibilities, have expertise and experience in construction project design review and evaluation, construction mobilization and supervision, bid evaluation, project scheduling, cost-benefit analysis, claims review and negotiation, and general management and administration of a construction project.[34]

§ 3.2   Key Clauses in Design Agreements

Typically, an architect engineer ("A/E") agreement is negotiated well before the owner-contractor agreement. As a result, the terms and conditions of the A/E agreement may substantially limit the flexibility of the owner in drafting the general owner-contractor agreement.

For example, entering into an AIA B-141 agreement with an architect may bind a city to use a specific set and edition of general terms and conditions, such as the AIA A-101 and AIA A-201 General Conditions. An A/E agreement is complementary to and administered in conjunction with a specific owner-contractor agreement. Thus, substantial differences in the terminology and scope of the architect-owner and owner-contractor agreement can result in major conflicts during the course of a project.

As a result, a common set of documents, such as AIA or EJCDC forms, is often used in the development of the A/E agreement. In addition, A/E's dealing with public agencies are extremely wary of E/O claims. Customarily, their errors and omissions (E/O) insurance carriers believe public entities and contractors are prone to making claims against design professionals. Therefore, architecture and engineering firms spend considerable amounts of time and effort negotiating contracts with public entities that contain a variety of limitations of liability, some reasonable and some not.

It is also important that essential legal issues, such as ownership and future use of the drawings, site field inspections, indemnification, and insurance be covered in these agreements, since design errors leading to structural failure, re-work, and late completion can result in millions of dollars of damage to the public entity.

When drafting or negotiating agreements with or on behalf of design professionals, one should understand the fundamental design contract issues. The following are key issues in design services agreements and a discussion of some of the rules that have been applied in resolving them.

§ 3.2(a) Project Description and Scope of Work

The project description should provide the main elements that define the limitations of the project, (i.e., purpose of structure, budget, square feet, number of floors, exterior skin), and it should disclaim inclusion of any excluded elements, (such as landscaping or lighting) that might otherwise be assumed to be included in a typical project of the same type. The scope of work should define the tasks, assignments, responsibilities, and other duties that will be included in the basic services and should specifically exclude those that are not included.

While the A/E may not actually be held liable for negligence where the scope of work is unclear, such a situation may cause serious deterioration of the relationship with the client and leave the A/E uncompensated for extra services performed.[35]

§ 3.2(b) Basic Services Versus Additional Services

It is important to differentiate between Basic Services and other services. Basic Services are included in the fixed-fee structure of an agreement, whereas additional services may require additional compensation. The A/E generally has the obligation to perform the basic services without obtaining advance approval but will often be required to obtain approval from the owner before performing additional services. A comprehensive treatment of this subject is found in AIA B 141, Article 2, titled "Scope of Architect's Basic Services," and in Article 3.

§ 3.2(c) Standard of Care

The A/E will be subject to the professional negligence standard of care unless the contract provides for a higher standard.[36] The owner may want to require a higher standard, such as that provided in the following provision excerpted from a public design contract drafted by a city attorney:

"The architect shall perform the professional services in accordance with the highest professional standards of those architects practicing in the [designated locale] area and engaged in providing [designated type of services] design and construction services."

This clause increases the duty of care to the highest standard, rather than the normal or ordinary standard, and defines the standard further by geographical area and subject matter. It is also arguably uninsurable, since typical A/E liability insurance only covers professional negligence, rather than adherence to the highest standard of practice in the area.

Some owners desire to obtain a further express warranty from the A/E despite the fact that the law does not do so; and, in professional practice, it is not realistic to provide such a warranty. Professional services have been consistently treated differently from products which are typically guaranteed.[37]

For a project with a unique or special use, the parties may specify the standard of care for that project. Otherwise, the professional standard of care does not require the A/E to guarantee the result or outcome of design or impliedly warrant the sufficiency of plans and specifications or their fitness for the project's intended use.[38] A contract that obligates the A/E to design a plant or equipment that will meet specified production parameters expressly set forth therein will be enforced as an express warranty of the design.[39]

§ 3.2(d) Schedule of Performance

Traditionally, A/Es do not have binding schedules in their professional services agreements. Where no time is specified for performance of a contract, a reasonable time is usually implied. Where the owner states that time is of the essence, any delay in the performance of the contract may constitute a material breach if it causes prejudice or harm to the owner. Generally, however, the quality of the A/E's performance is more critical than the timing of the performance.

The A/E's timeliness becomes critical once the construction portion of the project is awarded. The contractor and its subcontractors are contractually bound to the milestones and times set forth for construction agreement. The A/E is not contractually obligated to achieve the critical path or bound to those milestones, but the A/E's acts or omissions can affect whether the parties to the construction contract can meet their obligations.

§ 3.2(e) Redesign without cost

The owner is generally liable to the contractor for increases in the contract price associated with the cost of constructing or remedying work arising from the A/E's errors and omissions because, although the A/E does not guarantee the plans and specifications to the owner, the owner does guarantee them to the contractor for contract pricing purposes.[40]

The foregoing rule is separate from the A/E's liability for negligence, *i.e.*, injuries to persons or property caused by errors and omissions. It should be recognized that a contract clause stating that the A/E does not warrant or guarantee the plans and specifications, but that any errors or omissions in the drawings will be corrected by the A/E without additional cost to the owner, is a fairly restrictive form of limitation of liabilities, and is likely to be closely scrutinized regarding its enforceability.

§ 3.2(f) Adherence to Codes

The A/E is obligated to keep informed of building restrictions and regulations and to prepare plans and specifications that conform to building codes.[41] The A/E may be liable for violations of the Uniform Building

Code under the doctrine of negligence per se, which creates a presumption of due care and shifts the burden to the A/E to defend its conduct.[42]

Mere deviations from customary practice do not constitute negligence.[43] Complying with special industry standards or utilizing state-of-the-art technology may not be required to satisfy the standard of professional practice. The following provision excerpted from a public design contract drafted by another city attorney addresses this issue:

> The architect shall study all applicable laws (all codes, ordinances, rules, orders, regulations, and statutes affecting the project, including, but not limited to, tax codes, lien laws, zoning ordinances, environmental regulations, fire and safety codes and coverage, and density ratios) and comply with them in the performance of all the architect's professional services.

§ 3.2(g) Licensure and Payment

All persons preparing plans, specifications, and instruments of service for others must sign those documents and all associated contracts therein and, if licensed, must note their license numbers.[44] Generally, an unlicensed A/E cannot recover on a contract or for services rendered. However, a licensed person may recover on an implied, oral, or unsigned contract, or a contract that did not bear the A/E's license number where the A/E is licensed and is not alleged to have performed defective work.[45] Section 143 was recently added to Business and Professional Code and precludes professionals needing to be licensed thereunder from recovering where they are not licensed. The A/E may forfeit its right to payment for services for failure to prepare plans and specifications that conform to building codes.[46]

The owner may not refuse payment of costs due to alterations made during the course of construction[47] or changes made to the plans after a successful bidder has been located to do the work at the estimated price.[48] Where the contract makes payment dependent on a condition, the owner may not avoid payment by controlling the occurrence of that condition.[49]

If the contract expresses the measure of the A/E's compensation, the fee will be determined in accordance with the contract provisions.[50] If no provision is made as to compensation, the A/E is entitled to the reasonable value of the services.[51] This value may be determined by reviewing customary charges for similar services by other A/Es.

Where the A/E is terminated for convenience prior to completion of the project, the owner must pay for services rendered and expenses incurred to date of termination, unless the contract provides otherwise.[52]

Where the fee is based on a percentage of the construction cost, the contract should state explicitly whether that means the percentage of the construction cost anticipated at the time the A/E is terminated or the actual cost of the completed project.[53]

§ 3.2(h) Construction/Site Services–Shop Drawing & Submittal Review

The A/E is typically required to review and approve the contractor's submittals of shop drawings, samples, and other data for conformance with the conceptual design of the project and compliance with the information in the contract documents. However, these reviews do not include the means, methods, techniques, sequences, or procedures of construction or safety programs incident thereto.

Conflict often arises over the level of review given and the meaning of the A/E's approval. The contracts generally state that the A/E will review the submittals only for general conformance with the design concepts and that the A/E is not required to ensure the contractor's submittals are free from minor errors or deviations from specific requirements of the plans and specifications. When the contract delineates such responsibility, the A/E will not be held liable for the contractor's deviations from clear and specific requirements of the plans and specifications. Where a rigorous level of review and approval is desired, the contract should provide for adequate compensation and time for the A/E and its consultants to perform an indepth, quality assurance review.

§ 3.2(i) Construction Services– Change Order Evaluation and Approval

A major responsibility for A/Es who review and approve contractor change order requests is to ensure prompt negotiation of time and pricing adjustments. It is not common for the A/E to have the authority to bind the public works owner on change orders; therefore, the A/E should act in a manner that does not incur unnecessary delay or expense. For example, notice requirements, such as providing written notice of the nature and extent of a problem and its cost and schedule impact, must be observed and enforced, since by inaction or acquiescence, the A/E can waive the owner's right to written notice.[54]

When possible, the A/E should obtain advance agreements on changes, known as "forward priced change orders," to minimize the volume of unsettled claims. These may be based on the engineer's best estimate of costs, overhead, and profit for the work or can be unit prices based on industry averages. This technique eliminates the buildup of major financial arguments throughout the work and reduces the level of distrust that can exist where change orders are left up in the air.

The A/E is usually not empowered to create a new contract between the owner and the contractor under the guise of interpreting the original contract provisions or issuing change orders. The A/E must translate the contract and ascertain its intended meaning based on the original contract documents.

§ 3.2(j) Construction Services–Substitutions

One function of the A/E under traditional contracts is to evaluate and determine the acceptability of substitutions of materials or equipment proposed by contractors for materials or equipment specified in the contract documents. The A/E must review requests for substitution within a reasonable time period and must be fair and reasonable in approving or denying them.

Where the A/E's decision has a reasonable basis, it will usually be binding and final. The A/E may be liable for insistence on an exclusionary specification that cannot be performed by the successful bidder.[55]

§ 3.2(k) Construction Services–Supervision and Site Safety

The design professional's degree of responsibility for the safety of site contractors has been vigorously debated for the past three decades. As the contractual limitations of privity gave way to extended tort duties in the late 1950s, injured workers argued that the A/E's power to reject and stop work and provide general supervision gave them a responsibility to ensure site safety. Design professionals argued that their responsibility at a site was to monitor construction only on behalf of the owner, and only for general observation that the key design elements were being faithfully executed. As a result, strict contractual delineations of duties and disclaimers of site safety responsibility became fixtures in design professionals' contracts. Some courts have upheld such delineations of duty.[56]

However, if an A/E undertakes responsibility for safety in its contract with the owner, the contract becomes the initiating source of duty, and that duty is also extended to third parties.[57] Some courts have found that professionals may acquire a duty to third parties for safety—even though their contract does not give them such responsibility—if they assume that responsibility by conducting safety meetings, touring the site, and noting safety violations and unsafe practices.[58]

In the absence of an express assumption of safety responsibilities by contract or conduct, the modern view of the A/E's limited role, as stated in the California Architect's Practice Act, will prevail. The act specifically provides that construction observation "does not mean the superintendence of construction processes, site conditions, operations, equipment, or personnel, or the maintenance of a safe place to work or any safety in, on, or about the site.[59]

§ 3.2(l) Construction Services—Site Visits & Observation of Construction

The design professional's role at a site has also created a vigorous debate over the extent of the inspection of the contractor's work, the purpose of the inspection, and any resulting liability for defective work. The general rule is that where the A/E's contract imposes a duty to inspect the work or the A/E undertakes such a responsibility by its actions, the A/Es will be liable to the client and third parties for negligence in performing that work.[60]

By statute, architects do not have a duty to observe the construction of works for which they provide plans and specifications, but they may, by contract, agree to provide such services. Under the California Architect's Practice Act, those services are defined as "periodic observation of completed work to determine general compliance with the plans, specifications, reports, or other contract documents."[61] Therefore, if greater responsibility for inspections is desired, the degree to which the services are to extend beyond the normal A/E's role must be specified.

§ 3.2(m) Construction Services—Certification of Progress Payments

The architect must exercise care in the certification and payment process, where the architect approves the contractor's payment requests on the owner's behalf. Depending on the architect's scope of responsibility, liability may arise from certifying incorrect amounts for payment, not discovering defects in the work during inspections incidental to the certification process, issuing certificates without determining whether the contractor has paid its subcontractors and suppliers, not requiring lien waivers, and causing delays. As with other areas of the A/E's responsibility, the disputes revolve around the extent to which the A/E has responsibility, by contract or otherwise, for the contractor's poor performance or failure to perform.

The A/E may not withhold a certificate unreasonably,[62] and, absent fraud or mistake, the A/E's approval or certification of payment is generally final. In one fraud case, an owner recovered from the architect because the architect was also working for the contractor on another project at the time the certificate of payment was issued, creating a conflict of interest that justified setting aside the certificate.[63]

§ 3.2(n) Construction Services—Authority to Reject Work

The contract documents should clearly express the extent to which the owner wants the A/E to have the final decision on rejecting the contractor's work as defective or nonconforming. Presumably, since the contract documents reflect the A/E's design intent, the A/E should have the final say as to what was intended. However, giving the A/E the authority to reject or stop work exposes the A/Es to the contractor's claims of interference with the contract or economic advantage. Since this is an intentional tort, carrying with it the possibility of a greater measure of damages, it is a risk that should be minimized by clear expressions of authority and responsibility in the contracts. Unless the A/E's conduct is malicious or exceedingly unfair, the A/E will normally be protected by the quasi judicial immunity that cloaks its decisions when acting in the role of the arbiter of the contract between the contractor and the owner.[64] It is doubtful this immunity exists where the architect or engineer has a personal interest in the outcome or where it involves a design error when the designer may have personal responsibility.

§ 3.2(o) Construction Services—Substantial Completion & Final Payment

Improper declaration that the work is substantially complete, which supports the release of the final payment, raises similar issues as improper certification of progress payments, since the contractor receives funds meant to secure its performance. Where the items to be corrected or completed are punch list items instead of major incomplete or defective components of the project, the A/E should advise withholding a reasonable sum to assure performance of outstanding punch list items and release the remainder.

§ 3.2(p) Construction Services—Arbiter of Disputes

The A/E has three different roles in relation to the traditional construction contract: (1) independent contractor in the preparation of plans and specifications, (2) agent of the owner during construction contract administration, and (3) quasi-judicial officer with certain immunity when acting as the arbiter in resolving disputes between the owner and the contractor.[65] These roles should be clearly understood by the owner and contractor at the outset of a project. It is therefore advisable to include language in the contract referring to the differing responsibilities and liabilities when the A/E acts in these different roles.

§ 3.2(q) Cost Estimates

The A/E is often asked to provide the owner with opinions of probable project costs, which generally include construction costs and allowances for other related costs. Costs of land acquisition and rights-of-way, interest and financing charges, and other services provided by others are usually not evaluated by the A/E. Claims against the A/E for errors in estimated costs have produced mixed results. Generally, unless cost estimates are expressly warranted or result from fraud, the A/E is not liable for errors if the cost estimates are reasonably made.[66] The A/E is not liable if the owner has been notified that the project cannot be built for the estimated price and the owner proceeds, or where the owner's directives cause an increase in costs.[67]

The contract should clearly establish that opinions regarding construction or project costs are merely opinions for planning and design development purposes and are not guarantees. Where the owner seeks fixed cost estimates, estimates by the A/E should be verified by a contractor or professional cost estimator.

§ 3.2(r) Ownership, Use, and Reuse of Drawings

There is a fundamental difference in the ways design professionals and owners view the written work product generated during the design process. Owners want to protect their unique designs from replication or may desire confidentiality and control over the design process. They may also have other motives, such as the desire to minimize the A/E's involvement, and hence the fee, once the design has been completed. Design professionals, on the other hand, are interested in the authorship of their creative works and seek to minimize liability for the exposure resulting from the future use, misuse, modification, or misapplication of their drawings and other documents. The public also has an interest when construction drawings bearing an engineer's or architect's seal are used for another project without professional review or adaptation.

A further problem arises to the extent owners see A/Es as providers of products consisting of the designs embodied in the drawings and specifications, while designers see themselves as providers of building design services. The owners' perception may be at odds with the legal treatment of design professionals' work as well as with the nature of the work itself.

Most standard agreements provide that an A/E's written documents are instruments of the A/E's services and that the A/E retains all rights in them. Where an owner desires a different rule, the contract should balance the competing interests to make sure that the A/E is protected by receiving credit and compensation for the work, but not retaining liability for later use or misuse.

Owners often request protection of proprietary information or trade secrets that design professionals necessarily become familiar with while performing their services. All parties may desire confidential treatment of financial information that is exchanged to demonstrate the parties' ability to proceed. Such agreements are generally subject to exceptions where they may be required to disclose information, but they are generally upheld. Such exclusions commonly include information already in the public domain, in the possession of the other party prior to disclosure, information obtained from third parties not subject to a confidentiality agreement, or information required to be disclosed by public regulatory agencies.

§ 3.2(s) Copyrights and Patents

Since the enactment of the 1990 Architectural Works Copyright Protection Act, A/Es have enjoyed explicit copyright protection for the design elements in their work.[68] However, for developmental, research, or experimental work involving the design of a novel structure, process, or equipment owners often request a clause giving the owner all patent rights and copyrights.

§ 3.2(t) Indemnification

Indemnification is the contractual shifting of risk. It often is shifted by the stronger party who drafts the contract onto the weaker party who bids on the job. Generally, the clause will require one party to defend and pay the resulting loss. It is a craft area requiring special expertise and a knowledge of Civ. Code § 2782 that places limits on the extent that construction participants can shift the risk of loss to others, particularly where the indemnifying party is solely at fault or supplies defective designs.

§ 3.2(u) Insurance

A typical contract requires the A/E to maintain certain types of insurance coverage with specified limits, deductibles, and coverage features. It is important that the requirements can be fulfilled by the A/E in the commercial insurance marketplace. In general, the A/E's insurance should be at least $2 million, or 20 percent of the project value, whatever is greater.[69]

§ 3.2(v) Payment Bonds and Retention

Design professionals are rarely asked for payment bonds. Occasionally, they are asked for retention provisions. Retention provisions are usually a matter of negotiation.

§ 3.2(w) Suspension or Termination of A/E

If no contract clause governs the parties' rights to terminate the contract, the common law requires the examination of many factors to determine whether it is fair to allow termination.[70] These factors are the impact of the reason for termination (breach of conduct) on the non-breaching party, the likelihood of further breaches, whether the breach can be compensated by damages, the effect on the breaching party and the likelihood of losses or forfeitures on it, the likelihood that the breach can be cured, and the reason for the breach. Since termination disputes are resolved on a case-by-case basis, different facts lead to different outcomes. For example, in a case where the owner breached by failing to make payment, the court held that the contractor could rescind and recover the reasonable value of the work done.[71]

§ 3.3 STATUTES OF LIMITATION AND REPOSE

Often the A/E attempts to limit the time duration of its legal liability, say to 1, 3, or 5 years. As discussed in Section 14.4 and elsewhere, there already exist significant time limitations on claims. The California statutes generally applicable to actions involving A/Es are contained in the California Code of Civil Procedure § 335 *et seq*[72] Among the statutes are special provisions that apply to claims against public entities[73] and to actions based upon exposure to asbestos.[74] The statutes that provide the A/E the most substantive protection are the special construction industry statutes of repose.[75] They bar claims asserted more than four or ten years after substantial completion for patent or latent deficiencies, respectively. Additional protection is extended to trades and professions, such as architecture and engineering, such that "substantial completion" means when the tradespeople and professionals finish their work before the substantial completion of the entire improvement work.[76] These statutes have been generally upheld against constitutional attack on grounds of equal protection.[77] (also see Chapter 14)

Chapter 4

STANDARD CONTRACTS

The Old Placer County Courthouse, Auburn
Courtesy University of California Library, Davis California

Summary:

Typical contract documents used in the construction phase of private and public works projects are described. In addition, the various types of contracts are discussed in detail, including standard agreements, design agreements, general contractor agreements, and design-build agreements. The key clauses of agreements are outlined and include information on insurance coverage, licensing, bonding (including performance and payment bonds), wage rates, labor and materials provisions and warranty provisions. Specialized issues in design contracts are also addressed. In addition, the public sector's utilization of design-build with privatization is discussed, as well as the types of projects covered under California's Infrastructure Financing Act.

§ 4.1 INTRODUCTION

The purpose of this chapter is to provide a general understanding of the various contract provisions that must be considered for inclusion in a public works construction contract. Keep in mind that most public entities utilize a standard in-house contract document (including general conditions), as will be discussed later, and little room is allowed for negotiation by the construction professional, (the contractor or architect) regarding a public works contract.

The sections that follow include a description of the various contract documents typically used for public projects and a discussion of the types of contracts. A construction contract contains various documents commonly referred to jointly as the "contract documents." These documents may consist of bidding documents, the owner-contractor agreement, general conditions, supplementary conditions and/or special conditions, drawings and technical specifications, standard specifications, reference specifications, addenda, and modifications. These individual documents cross-reference each other in order to form the contract. The next few paragraphs briefly describe these contract documents.

1. Bidding documents typically include an invitation to bid, instructions to the bidder (including an affidavit of non-collusion), and bid forms (the bidding process is discussed in detail in Chapter 8).

2. The owner-contractor agreement consists of five elements, including the identity of the parties, description of the work to be performed, time for performance, contract price, and payment schedules.

3. The general conditions provide additional scope and detail and expressly state the various responsibilities, rights, and duties of the parties. These conditions are usually standard provisions provided in all construction contracts and are not project specific. The Standard Specifications for Public Works Construction (1997) and other standard contract documents provide for such general conditions.[78]

4. Supplementary and/or special conditions are inserted for specific reasons, usually to provide for special circumstances or conditions unique to a particular project.

5. Drawings represent the actual layout, dimensions, and construction details of the project. They are utilized by the contractor to determine the quantity of material required for the project, as well as the cost of construction. More importantly, they are used by the contractor to con-

struct the project and usually include architectural, structural, mechanical, and electric drawings. The architect or engineer is responsible for preparing drawings or plans for the entire project.

6. Specifications are documents that supplement the drawings, providing detailed descriptions of various portions of the project. Technical specifications are the engineering description of the project and include testing information for the specific work to be completed. Standard specifications include boiler plate written descriptions of steel, concrete, materials, and so forth, that are common on almost every job. Reference specifications refer to accepted third-party specifications that are published by technical and engineering societies, public agencies, and other parties involved in numerous projects nationally. The engineer is typically responsible for preparing these specifications to conform with the project drawings.

7. Addenda are included to make changes prior to the execution of the basic owner-contractor agreement and are usually issued by the owner prior to bid acceptance.

8. Modifications are any substantial written changes to the owner-contractor agreement.

Several business terms must be kept in mind when drafting or choosing which provisions to include within a contract. A **fixed-price** or **lump-sum** contract involves a contractor agreeing to complete a project for a fixed price according to the contract documents. **Unit-price** contracts involve a fixed price per unit of material or quantity of work to be performed. **Cost-plus** or **force-account** contracts provide reimbursement for all costs of construction, plus a percentage amount to compensate for overhead and profit.

Public works contracts are interpreted in the same manner and under the same rules as are private contracts.[79] More important, however, is the application of the parol evidence rule, which provides that if a written contract is a complete and final expression of the parties (complete integration), any contrary, inconsistent, or conflicting prior agreements or statements will be inadmissible to vary the terms of the written agreement.[80] Thorough research and analysis of contract law in this area can yield important ruling precedent.

§ 4.2 "STANDARD AGREEMENTS"

Most construction contracts trace their ancestry from standard contract forms developed by the American Institute of Architects (AIA), Associated General Contractors of America (AGC), and Engineers Joint Contract Documents Committee (EJCDC). These are widely utilized within the public works departments of counties, cities, and special districts. Smaller cities and public agencies, especially special districts, use a variety of individually tailored forms that often incorporate major provisions of the construction industry professional groups listed above.

In California, the most commonly encountered public works contracts are (1) California Department of Transportation Contracts; (2) State of California Department of General Services Contracts; (3) Southern California Contract and Specifications (Greenbook editions); and (4) standard construction contracts of various large cities and counties.

A fairly high degree of standardization exists for contracts in categories 1, 2, and 3, above. The remaining contracts issued by California public entities are apt to contain clauses and provisions unique to the specific projects.

This patchwork quilt of "standard" agreements creates difficulties for both public agencies and the private contracting community. Contractors rarely make pre-bid comments regarding contractual provisions. They should do so when those provisions place unnecessary burdens on their operations or require disproportionate contingencies. Since these contractual provisions are issued to the bidding community largely on a "take it or leave it" basis, it is rare that a city or agency will have an opportunity to know the cost or scheduling impacts of various provisions included in its contracts.

In contrast to the private construction environment, where a contractor can negotiate various provisions in exchange for reductions in price and other concessions, the public entity may incorporate certain clauses without realizing their impact. For example, excessive liquidated damages provisions may substantially increase the cost of the job without providing substantial benefit for a city or county.

While general contractors can theoretically suggest changes to contracts through requests for clarification or requests for an addendum on a particularly onerous clause, changes rarely happen. Thus, public entities must be careful not to draft contracts that are so protective of the owner that the number of bidders is few and the ultimate project costs are unnecessarily inflated.

A typical approach to drafting a public works contract consists of three stages. First, the nature of the project needs to be defined, including the owner's and contractor's major risks. Second, a rough draft must be developed, often modeled on a contract for a similar project of like scope and magnitude. Lastly, the final agreement must be completed, incorporating comments from various operating divisions and professionals within the city or other public entity.

Review of a contract by legal counsel should include a thorough check of standard contract issues and required statutory public works and grant clauses.

Extreme rigor in preparing public works contracts and bidding documents is required, since contracts that (1) result from improper bid processes and/or (2) contain clauses that violate public policy or the grant documents may be found to be <u>null and void</u>. At a minimum, bid protests (discussed in Section 8.11) may substantially delay a project or force rebidding.

Generations of public entity attorneys have added increasingly sophisticated clauses and provisions that can work to the disadvantage of the general contractor. Attorneys are strongly urged to review in detail not only the special provisions but also the so-called boilerplate provisions of any contracts that do not contain pre-printed standardized general conditions that may have been subject to prior legal and commercial review. Commercial review means that business aspects of the project, including marketing issues and profit potential, as opposed to the technical or legal risk issues involved.

Finally, where a general contractor encounters clauses that pose unacceptably high risks and the public agency is unwilling to reconsider or modify those clauses, the contractor may decide to make a "no bid" decision. When this is done, it is generally appropriate for the contractor to notify the public entity regarding the offensive clause or clauses.

§ 4.3   Key Clauses in General Contractor Agreements

The Contract Code requires or allows certain clauses to be included in public works contracts. In addition, the code prohibits or limits the use of certain types of clauses that the state legislature has found violate public policy. Below are the major examples of each.

§ 4.3(a) Allowed Clauses

Two allowed clauses are "value engineering" and "differing site conditions" clauses.

A public entity may provide for the payment of extra compensation to a contractor for cost reduction changes in the plans and specifications. As an incentive to make technical changes in the work that result in a better project, at less cost, the contractor may be given a share of the cost savings under a value engineering contract provision. This is termed the value engineering clause. Value engineering clauses are allowed to offer up to 50 percent of the savings to the contractor.[81]

The differing site conditions clause pertains to public works projects that require trenches or excavations over four feet in depth. Agreements for such projects must provide for contractor notice and owner payment for (1) hazardous waste generated during the project, (2) physical conditions at the site differing from those outlined in the contract, and (3) unknown and unusual physical conditions.[82]

§ 4.3(b) Prohibited or Limited Clauses

When the owner creates an unreasonable delay, the contract may not preclude recovery of damages by the contractor or subcontractor. This type of clause is referred to as a damage for delay clause.[83]

A release of claims clause is also prohibited. This clause requires the release of any claims by a contractor in order to be paid undisputed contract amounts. However, a contract provision making the payment of an undisputed amount contingent upon the contractor providing to the public entity a release of claim form for that undisputed amount is not against public policy and thus is proper to include in a contract.[84]

Public contracts may not require contractors to be responsible for the cost of repairing damage to a project that is more than 5 percent of the contracted amount if the damage is caused by an Act of God. Such a requirement is called a force majeure clause. The term "Act of God" is very broad and difficult to define. Two obvious examples are extreme weather and earthquakes. However, what one party to the contract believes to be an Act of God may not be true for another party.[85]

The former use of "paid when paid" clauses in subcontracts has been found to be against public policy. These clauses allowed a general contractor to delay paying its subcontractors when there was a pending claim or delay problem. It also gave the general contractor the ability to argue that is was not liable to the subcontractors in the event of the default or bankruptcy of the owner.

The relevant case[86] was decided by the Supreme Court on June 26, 1997. Four subcontractors entered into agreements with the general contractor on a commercial building project. The subcontracts included "pay if paid" provisions, which made payment by the building owner to the general contractor a condition precedent to the general contractor's obligation to pay the subcontractors. Three of the four subcontracts purported to preserve the subcontractors' mechanic's lien rights. However, the general contractor obtained a payment bond from an insurer to protect the owner from mechanic's lien claims. After substantial work had been completed on the project, the building owner stopped making payments to the general contractor, who then declined to pay the subcontractors.

The subcontractors recorded mechanic's liens and filed actions against the surety. The trial court granted judgment for the subcontractors and against the surety.[87]

The court of appeal,[88] affirmed the decision of the trial court. The Supreme Court then affirmed the judgment of the court of appeal and remanded the case for further proceedings, holding that the surety was liable to the subcontractors on the payment bond and that a general contractor's liability to a subcontractor may not be made contingent on the owner's payment to the contractor.[89]

Although a "pay if paid" provision is not precisely a waiver of mechanic's lien rights, this type of provision has the same practical effect as an express waiver of those rights. Hence, it is void because it violates the public policy regarding the antiwaiver provisions of the mechanic's lien laws.[90] Since all but one of the subcontracts purported to preserve the mechanic's lien rights and remedies, enforcement of the "pay if paid" provisions would not have been consistent with the intent of the contracting parties.

In most cases, a general contractor is forced to enter into "liquidation agreements" with its subcontractors. These agreements, entered into after a dispute arises, allow the general contractor to delay paying the subcontractors, especially claim amounts, until the claim is resolved with the owner.

§ 4.3(c) Key Public Works Clauses

Many general provisions are required to be included in a public works contract document. Provisions relating to bonds, insurance, and licensing requirements are but a few of the provisions to consider inserting. These and other required provisions are discussed below.

- A contractor who is awarded a public works contract must post a payment bond with the public entity if the contract exceeds $25,000.[91]

- Typically, the public entity will require the contractor to submit proof of liability insurance with the public agency named as an additional insured. The AIA General Conditions contain standard insurance provisions.[92] Before entering into a public works contract, each party should speak with a knowledgeable broker specializing in construction insurance, as many general agents may be unaware of important coverage issues specific to the construction industry.

- Contractor licensing provisions[93] along with minority/disability business solicitation requirements[94] must be included in every public works contract. These requirements are more fully discussed in other areas of this manual.

- Contractors performing work on a public works project are required to pay prevailing wage rates, which are specified by the public entities in the bidding documents, as well as the contracts themselves.[95] In addition, clauses relating to permits and fees, conformity with applicable codes, site access and inspection, and scheduling requirements must be included in the public works contracts.

- Labor and materials provisions, extra work or change clauses (giving either party authority to modify or change the contract),[96] notice requirements, and delay and extensions clauses are essential in all public works contracts.

- Warranty provisions are essential as well, and both express and implied warranty issues should be considered. The duration of a warranty in the construction industry is typically one year. However, the expiration of a warranty period does not apply to defective construction, which amounts to a breach of contract. Such situations are governed by the statute of limitations, which is four years for breach of a written contract.[97]

- Indemnification,[98] claims procedures, termination and default on the contract, liquidated damages, arbitration, and attorneys' fees clauses[99] are other provisions that are included in the AIA General Conditions.

- As stated above, bond provisions are required in all public works contracts. Bonding requirements are important in that liens cannot be filed against public property. Prime contractors are required to post performance and payment bonds, which guarantee the faithful performance of the contract by the prime contractor and act as security for any claim that may arise from an unpaid subcontractor or material supplier.[100]

Litigation regarding payment bonds can be very protracted. A representative and important case is <u>Contractors Labor Pool, Inc. v. Westway Contractors, Inc.</u>[101] In this case, a company that provided workers to a subcontractor on a public works project brought an action to recover outstanding amounts after the subcontractor fell behind in its payments for the plaintiff's services. The trial court found that both the subcontractor and its president were liable to the plaintiff and that the plaintiff was entitled to recover against the payment bond on the project. In a post-judgment order, the court awarded the plaintiff costs and attorney fees.[102]

The court of appeal affirmed the judgment but remanded the matter for a redetermination of attorney fees and costs. The court of appeal held that the trial court did not err in finding that the plaintiff was entitled to recover on the project's payment bond. Those who furnish laborers for a public works project, as well as those who perform labor themselves, are entitled to recover against a payment bond. The plaintiff's status as an employer was the key to its right of recovery.

The court further held that the plaintiff was entitled to recover, notwithstanding Bus. & Prof. Code § 7031 (which states that a person engaged in contractor activities must be duly licensed in order to recover compensation for contractor services). The applicable rule was that a person or company in the business of supplying equipment or hiring out laborers to be supervised by others does not act in the capacity of a contractor and is therefore not required to have a license. Finally, the court held that the trial court erred in applying the restrictions of a local court rule in awarding attorney fees under Civil Code § 3250. To the extent the rule restricted the amount otherwise awardable under the statute, it was invalid.[103]

The Miller Act[104] applies to federal public works and requires government prime contractors to provide performance and payment bonds. This is similar to the California bonding requirements in Contract Code §§ 10221-10224 and § 20426.

§ 4.4 Design-Build Agreements

As previously mentioned, Design-build[105] is a project delivery system under which a single entity (known as the design-builder) is contractually responsible for *both* the design and construction of a project.

The design-builder is generally (1) a general contractor that employs its own architects or engineers or retains them on a consulting basis, or (2) a joint venture between a general contractor and a design firm. On rare occasions, the design-builder is an architecture or engineering firm that subcontracts the construction phase.

Design-build competes with the more established "*design-bid-build*" system, where design is completed separately prior to competitive bidding of the construction. This older approach, long used for private and public works, was established to produce facilities at the lowest cost to the public. Fierce competition has been fostered among contractors, each bidding a lump sum on an identical set of design documents.

Unlike manufacturing, where design and production are inseparable, the design-bid-construct model prides itself on the fact that the designer remains independent of the contractor. The designer is then expected to provide (1) an excellent design for the owner; (2) reasonable cost and schedule estimates; and (3) independent and objective inspection and enforcement of quality standards in the contract. Furthermore, the bid competition is thought to assure the lowest price for a fixed scope of work.

The lump-sum contract is by far the most common type of contract in the construction industry. In it, the contractor agrees to perform the specified work for a fixed price within a fixed time. If the cost of the work exceeds or falls below the fixed price, the contractor absorbs the loss or reaps the gain. Owners think they know exactly what services they will get before they agree on the price or start of construction.

Unfortunately, the result of the design-bid-construction approach can be a highly contentious jobsite. Designers may be isolated from the financial pressures of construction. Their cost and schedule estimates are notoriously inaccurate (and their E/O carriers exclude coverage for their attempts). They are unaware of newer construction means and methods, lack field experience and construction savvy, and therefore provide designs that are often unconstructable or outdated. While they are independent with regard to inspection, they are usually prohibited from conducting inspections by their E/O insurance carriers, which limit this valuable involvement to "observation from time to time of general construction progress."

Low-bid public projects, often with unclear and ambiguous plans, have fostered a significant number of serious contract disputes and litigation. As a result, owners, designers, and constructors have been pursuing alternative methods to make the interfaces in project delivery systems more workable. Design-build is an answer to these problems on selected projects.

While the U.S. public sector predominantly uses the design-bid-build project delivery system, the use of design-build is increasing. Firms such as Bechtel, Fluor Daniel, and other international constructors have long offered their clients this form of one-stop shopping on major projects in the nuclear, petrochemical, pharmaceutical, and industrial sectors. The public sector has used design-build for prisons, public and military housing, educational facilities, physical fitness facilities, warehouses, and other projects where the scope of work can be easily developed and replicated.

Recently, the public sector in California, specifically Cal Trans, has used design-build and privatization, an emerging public works management system, whereby the government contracts with a private entity to undertake some or all phases of the system that have traditionally been the responsibility of the government, including project financing, land acquisition, design, construction, and operation. Other landmark California design-build projects include the San Joaquin Transportation Corridor and the Eastern Transportation Corridor (Transportation Corridor Agencies, Santa Ana) and the high Occupancy Vehicle Lanes Project - State Route 91 (California Private Transportation Corporation, Orange and Riverside Counties).

Perhaps the most innovative and controversial recent statute is California's Infrastructure Financing Act which is intended to provide California public entities with new sources of private sector investment capital to design, construct, maintain, rebuild, repair, and operate revenue-generating public infrastructure facilities.[106] The act may be used by any California city and/or county (including a chartered city or county), school district, community college district, public district, county board of education, joint powers authority, transportation commission or authority, or any other public or municipal corporation.[107]

Covered infrastructure projects include the design, construction, or reconstruction by, and lease to, private entities for the following types of fee-producing infrastructure projects:

irrigation

drainage

energy or power production

water supply, treatment, and distribution

flood control

inland waterways

harbors

municipal improvements

commuter and light rail

highways or bridges

tunnels

airports and runways

purification of water

sewage treatment, disposal, and water recycling

refuse disposal

structures or buildings, except structures or buildings that are to be utilized primarily for sporting or entertainment events.[108]

Projects may be proposed by the private entity and selected by the government agency at the discretion of the agency. Projects may be proposed and selected individually or as a part of a related or larger project. The competitive negotiation process must utilize as the primary selection criteria the demonstrated competence and qualifications of the contractor for the studying, planning, design, development, financing, construction, maintenance, rebuilding, improvement, repair, or operation, or any combination thereof, of the facility.

The selection criteria must also ensure that the infrastructure facility is operated at fair and reasonable prices to the user of the facility's services. The competitive negotiation process can not require competitive bidding. The selection and contract award process is exempt from the California Environmental Quality Act (CEQA). However, the entity selected must proceed with CEQA compliance.

It is generally assumed that Proposition 218 does not apply to privatized infrastructure. Therefore, the California Infrastructure Financing

Act may be the only feasible alternative for many local projects where there is localized opposition to raising taxes or imposing new user fees. In addition, the approval of a variable user fee tied to the consumer price index, a long-term rate schedule, or a multiple of future, actual costs incurred in delivering the services may exempt local public entities from seeking future rate increases that may prove problematic under Proposition 218.

Among federal agencies, the U.S. Postal Service, the General Services Administration, and the U.S. Army Corps of Engineers utilize the design-build approach for significant portions of their construction procurement budgets.

Traditionally, the design professions have resisted design-build, perhaps out of fear that their professions would be marginalized by large, integrated, design-build firms led by general contractors. That resistance appears to be diminishing. As evidence of this change in attitude, the AIA has issued its own set of design-build documents, as discussed below. Additionally, in October 1994, the National Society of Professional Engineers (NSPE) issued a discussion paper on design-build in the public sector in which design-build is recognized as "an established and acceptable process."

In its recent issue brief entitled "Design-Build in the Public Sector,"[109] NSPE states,

> "In the public sector, design-build is used as a specialized delivery system in certain limited situations. The federal government's experience with design-build is rather recent. The U.S. Department of Defense has used design-build only since 1987, when it received authorization to do so under the Military Construction Act of 1986. Some civilian federal agencies are also using design-build under their federal acquisition authorities."

The principal benefit of design-build contracts to the owner is a single point of responsibility for both design and construction. In addition, design-build provides other benefits, as discussed below.

a) Cost

Project costs may be lower because of the close working relationship between designers and constructors. This may lead to the incorporation of more economical design features and the application of cost-saving construction methods.

b) Team Atmosphere

Projects may proceed more efficiently because designers and constructors are members of the same "team." The interface between designer and constructor, often adversarial within design-bid-build systems, may become more open and foster a cooperative exchange of ideas to produce a profitable project. When problems arise on a project, the owner will not be faced with an architect, construction manager, and contractor each blaming the others. The designer-builder takes the responsibility for completing the project according to the owner's requirements, on time, and within a guaranteed maximum price.

c) Efficiency

Construction efficiency may be improved because design efficiencies can be woven throughout the construction process and because the designer, as a member of the design-build team, can participate directly in resolving design issues that surface during construction.

d) Critical Flaw Analysis

The design-build team has a greater chance of seeing critical flaws in the design stage when they can be avoided or mitigated. These flaws comprise a broad array of design and construction risks that a joint team is better prepared to address than a designer alone.

e) Rapid Response on Design Issues

A design-build team can react faster and with more clarity when design flaws are noted or ambiguities arise. In the traditional design-bid-construction approach, the response to design flaws or ambiguities is often defensive and hostile. The design-build team must react immediately since it owns the problem and must therefore correct it immediately.

In a design-build project, the design professional, or the A/E, is not the owner's or agency's consultant, but rather the contractor's teammate. The team either negotiates or presents a competitive proposal for both the design and construction of a particular project. Design-build projects can be accomplished in a variety of formats:

- *The competitive lump sum pricing format* can be used with the design-build approach. Where this format is utilized, the lump sum price may be determined for the entire project in advance before the design phase is completed, or it may be split into a design fee and a construction cost, with the lump sum construction cost to be determined after the design phase is completed. Generally, lump sum jobs must have a clear definition of the project (*e.g.*, roadway plan and profile views) and a very exacting set of design guidelines for the design-builder to follow (*e.g.*, Cal Trans standards).

- *The negotiated price format* can be used to establish an initial design budget; then the scope and price of the project can be negotiated as the project design proceeds. Cost savings through value engineering, creative construction technologies, and scheduling efforts can be extremely significant.

- *The reimbursable cost format* can be used from the beginning of a project with both design and construction done according to pre-agreed rates and overhead markups. A *guaranteed maximum price* can be negotiated or bid at any time in the project.

- *Fast-track procedures* allow certain elements of construction to proceed concurrently with the design process. This method allows work on one element of a project to proceed prior to the designs for the structure being finalized. Fast-track procedures can overlap and compress the design and construction phases. Thus, the total time from conception to completion is greatly reduced. For example, the foundation or structural steel work may be released for bids prior to the completion of the building design or before bids are solicited on the electrical, plumbing, or heating, ventilation, and air conditioning (HVAC) work.

The design-build **selection process** is another issue that must be addressed. The owner may select the design-builder by (1) directly selecting sole source design-builders; (2) negotiating with a group of pre-qualified design-builders; or (3) soliciting lump sum proposals from design-builders through competitive bids.

Direct selection is typically used by a private owner. The owner will usually select the design-builder based on a past relationship between the parties or by the reputation of the design-builder. Thus, developing a design-build clientele requires marketing effort rather than just bidding.

When utilizing a negotiation approach to selecting a design-builder, the owner will usually use the same criteria as in a direct-select method, but will also consider fee, scheduling, and costs.

In public works projects, the selection approach is highly formalized. The owner may issue a "criteria" package and then issue requests for proposals (RFPs) to design-builders. The proposals or packages and costs are reviewed by a committee appointed by the public owner.

The criteria for selecting the best proposing design-builders varies from statute to statute, but generally includes successful performance of prior projects, resumes of project executives, the qualifications of the designers, financial strength, and whether the design-build team has worked together previously. The project is then awarded to the lowest successful bidder.

NSPE has advocated developing criteria for a two-step selection process. In the first step, the involved agency would select at least five offerers on the basis of their qualifications. In the second step, each of the offerers would be required to submit detailed proposals, including cost information. A single offerer would then be selected.

Another consideration of the selection process should be the use of model contracts. Until recently, the only model contract forms available for the design-build industry have been the AIA forms, specifically, AIA document A191, Standard Form of Agreement between Owner and Design-Builder. Recently, however, the AGC published families of model contracts for design-build projects. These model contract forms are extremely helpful in establishing the legal relationships between the various project parties. For example, the AGC now has available AGC Document 420, Standard Form of Agreement between Contractor and Architect/Engineer for Design-Build Projects.

Of course, it is always important to remember that using the model contracts can have significant legal consequences. It is recommended that a design-builder always consult with an attorney before use or modifications of these documents.

More important in the selection process are the model code considerations. In order to promote the more widespread and consistent use of design-build by public agencies, the American College of Construction Lawyers (ACCL) and the Building Futures Council (BFC) developed the Design-Build Model Procurement Code for adoption by state and local governments. It provides an excellent first step toward establishing criteria, soliciting proposals, and making awards. It is expected that many states will consider adopting the model code, which will result in the uniform and consistent implementation of design-build procurement procedures.

Several other design-build statutes are applicable to California public works projects. Yet, many public agencies consider themselves re-stricted in using design-build contracts. Until recently, most public agencies required competitive bidding and awarded contracts to the lowest responsible bidder.[110] However, exceptions exist to the state's competitive bidding requirements, for example, contracts with pri-vate architecture and engineering firms.[111] In addition, some public agencies utilizing joint exercise of powers agreements, under which a project is constructed according to an agreement between two or more public agencies, may construct such projects without competi-tive bidding.[112]

Further, California authority provides that the Department of General Service (DGS) may enter into design-build agreements for office and parking facilities.[113] Government Code § 17827.3 exempts those con-tracts from competitive bidding when DGS decides that the state's best interest would be served by that exemption.

Projects that are exempt from the Contract Code include those con-struction or improvement projects whose costs are less than $25,000. Other exemptions include emergency work[114] and specialized per-sonal services (*e.g.*, the services of architects, engineers, land sur-veyors, and construction project management services).[115]

More important to the design-build industry, competitive bidding is not required *when it fails to produce an advantage and when the ad-vertisement for competitive bids is undesirable, impractical, or impos-sible.*[116] For example, in <u>Graydon</u> the court rejected the need for competitive bidding, stating that if the municipality had complied with competitive bidding requirements, a 14-month delay in construction probably would have resulted, substantially impairing the municipality's ability to repay the bond issue that was used to finance the construc-tion. The court went on to say that where it is practically impossible to obtain what is required and to observe such form, competitive bid-ding is not applicable.

In 1989, the California legislature enacted statutes to empower Cal Trans to contract with private developers to construct and operate tollway facilities under lease agreements with the state.[117] These stat-utes arose from a legislative determination that "public sources of revenues to provide an efficient transportation system have not kept pace with California's growing transportation needs, and alternative funding sources should be developed to augment or supplement available public sources of revenue."

In Professional Engineers in California Government v. Department of Transportation,[118] the court reviewed Assembly Bill 680 and the agreements between Cal Trans and the private developers. The court found that where letting of any service contract or franchise might open the door to the spoils system, the legislature can adopt other measures to prevent such abuse. Further, the court found that to discourage this type of experimentation would denigrate a key purpose of the civil service mandate – to promote efficiency and economy in state government.

The risks involved with the design-build approach apply to both the contractor and the public agency owner. The most apparent risk for the contractor is inflation of the scope and quality of a project and resultant impacts on cost and schedule. In a typical construction contract, the contractor is usually entitled to a change order when there has been a change to the scope of work, changed conditions, or errors or omissions in the plans and/or specifications. In a design-build contract, the design-builder may be entitled to a change order when the owner requests certain changes in scope or when unforeseen conditions are encountered; but, since the design-builder is responsible for the design, plans, and specifications, it cannot claim entitlement to a change order as a result of its own error or omission.

Once the design-builder assumes the responsibility for design, it also assumes the responsibility for the accuracy of the drawings and specifications. However, a general contractor who has contracted for the design services may bring an E/O claim against its design firm partner or consultant, depending on the contract.

For the owner, the combination of the designer and the builder contractor may result in a sacrifice in the owner's ability to control the design. Additionally, the checks and balances inherent in the owner-designer-builder relationship are largely eliminated.

Another area of concern for the owner is design and construction quality. When the design professional serves as an employee or subcontractor of the design-builder, conflicts may arise between the design professional's duty to its immediate employer or client and an independent duty to the owner. Also, more opportunities exist for the design-builder to lower the quality of the plans, specifications, and other areas, often in subtle ways that the owner may not be able to easily detect.

Insurance and liability are other key issues that must be addressed in the design-build context. A designer may be hesitant to participate in a design-build project because of the increased liability exposure. Such exposure includes the presence of guaranty/warranty clauses in de-sign-build contracts.

Ordinarily, an engineer (or architect) is held responsible only for exer-cising the degree of skill or care that the average, similarly situated engineer would employ and does not warrant or guarantee a suc-cessful outcome for its services.

The design-build contractor should keep in mind that insurance cov-erage for the design-build team is generally a manuscript-type cover-age negotiated with the insurance carrier for the specific project. Similarly, contract language, particularly guaranty/warranty and insur-ance provisions, must be specially drafted to fit the situation or project.

Lastly, the following are but a few of the specialized issues addressed in design-build contracts:

Design Approvals	Design Standards
Description of Services	Party Responsibilities
Construction (Requirements)	Operation and Maintenance
Design Fee	Contract Price
Dispute Resolution	Finance/Payments
Indemnification	Bonding
Insurance	Warranties
Changes/Extra Work	Suspension of Services
Default	Acceptance

Chapter 5

SPECIAL ATTRIBUTES OF PUBLIC WORKS PROJECTS

Sonoma County Courthouse, Santa Rosa
Photo by Robert Brekke

Summary:
Each and every public works project in California is unique. To complicate matters further, each of the 7,000 public entities in California have separate rules regarding construction projects. The author explains the three purposes for established policy awarding public projects to the lowest "responsible" bidder. The California Codes and some U.S. Federal laws governing state and local public works are cited and discussed. An overview of the Contract Code is broken down into three sections and the section's contents explained and reviewed. This chapter also discusses Contract Code Section 10115, which assists the interests of minority, women, and disabled veteran enterprises.

§ 5.1 PUBLIC AGENCY CONTRACT ADMINISTRATION

Every individual public works project is **unique** in California. That is certainly the experience of any general contractor or lawyer who is experienced in these type of projects. Not only are these projects administratively different from private projects conducted in this state, they are completely individualistic in legal content and administrative style from projects undertaken in other states or under contract with the federal government.

Even more mind boggling, **each public entity** in California has **separate rules** regarding construction projects. No two are the same. That is what makes California public works fun and interesting.

It is hard to imagine, yet more than 7,000 public entities exist in California, including the state of California, counties, cities, and myriad types of special districts. It is important to note that while many of these entities are required to adhere to some aspect of the Public Contract Code, almost all of them also have agency-specific regulations, ordinances, and charters, as well as a variety of internal (written and unwritten) procedures governing public works contracts and dispute resolution. Regardless of the exact rules, however, virtually all address the same issues covered in this manual. They just treat them uniquely.

There are substantial differences between the administration of these public projects and the private market. Public funds are administered through agencies run by elected officials. The main purpose of public procurement statutes is to provide the public with the best quality of project at the best price through a fair, efficient, and clear bidding process. Public agencies and administrators are not given unfettered discretion as to the award and administration of public projects, and contractors are held to exacting standards of performance once a project is underway.

In the not so distant past, political processes were substantially affected by campaign contributions tied to the award of public projects. However, as a result of public outcry for financial accountability in federal, state, and local public works projects, legal reforms have occurred and comprise the core of current public contract law and administration.

The most comprehensive compilation of regulations regarding public

54

works construction is found in the Public Contract Code. Although numerous other statutes affect the construction industry, the Public Contract Code was specifically drafted to protect public taxpayer funds from fraud and abuse and to provide for fair and efficient administration of public works projects. The Public Contract Code consists of two volumes and is supplemented annually.

Under the Public Contract Code, projects conducted via State of California and local agency contracts are fully designed with approved plans and specifications, and contracts are awarded after competitive bidding by large general contractors with surety bonds guaranteeing their performance and payment obligations. The general rule of California Public Works Contracting is to award the lowest responsible and responsive bidder after open competitive bidding.

While the techniques of design-build, multiple prime contracts, performance specifications, force account and other contracting methods are authorized for special circumstances, these techniques are still exceptions to the rule. However, in the past ten years, the California State Legislature has passed numerous specialized statutes providing exceptions to this rule. The principal exception to the rule, the design-build approach, is discussed in Section 5.4.

The policy of awarding public projects to the lowest responsible bidder has three purposes: (1) to eliminate favoritism, fraud, and corruption by political officials and their staffs in the awarding of public contracts; (2) to obtain highly competitive prices for public improvements; and (3) to provide a "level playing field" so that all qualified and bonded contractors in the state of California may bid on projects for which they are qualified.

We now cover the most important Public California codes and a few U.S. federal laws governing state and local public works.

§ 5.2 Overview of the Public Contract Code

The Public Contract Code is broken down into three sections: (1) administrative provisions, consisting of definitions of specific terms and the purpose of the Public Contract Code; (2) contracting by state agencies; and (3) contracting by local agencies, including school districts, general law cities and counties, and special districts. These three sections are discussed next.

§ 5.2.1 Administrative Provisions

The Public Contract Code states that the purpose of public contract law is primarily to clarify and ensure full compliance with competitive bidding requirements, but also "to eliminate favoritism, fraud, and corruption in the awarding of public contracts."[121] Public Contract Code § 102 encourages uniformity in public contract law to encourage competition for public contracts and to aid public officials in administering these contracts. Section 102 is extremely useful regarding the applicability of actions and interpretations of other public agencies as precedent. Public agencies are strongly encouraged to review the reported decisions for guidance.

The Public Contract Code applies to contracting by a "public entity." The definition of "public entity" includes "the state, county, city, city and county, district, public authority, public agency, municipal corporation, or any other public subdivision or public corporation in the state."[122] A "Public Works Contract" is defined as "an agreement for the erection, construction, alteration, repair, or improvement of any public structure, building, road, or other public improvement of any kind."[123]

As stated in § 1.0 of this manual, not all portions of the Public Contract Code apply to every public agency. In fact, much of the effort and analysis of public contract disputes is devoted to determining which provisions apply to the specific agency in question.

In the past, the Public Contract Code permitted local agencies to set guidelines regarding minority, women and disabled participation goals, good faith efforts and percentage goals,[124] and certification of minority and women business enterprises,[125] all of which were intended to foster equal opportunity.[126] The courts and California Proposition 209 have severely restricted the application of these types of statutes in State of California contracting, and many cases challenging such statutes are still on appeal. However, it appears clear that most state and local agencies will continue to seek opportunities to promote the success of minority-owned and woman-owned businesses by direct and indirect encouragement.

So that only legally qualified contractors bid on a project, the Public Contract Code requires a public agency to specify the necessary contractor's license classification in its bid invitations.[127] The contractor directly contracted with the public agency is the only one subject to the general contractor licensing classification requirement. (*See* Chapter 7 for further discussion of this topic.)

In preparing its bid documents, a public agency is permitted to request a brand name or specific product manufacturer in the bidding documents. However, to foster competition, the contractor may generally request an exception to specified brand names. Special provisions (so-called "Or Equal" provisions) govern the circumstances under which contractors may substitute materials or equipment for those specified.[128] The most important provision is that a contractor is allowed to substitute the particular named product only with a product of equal quality and likeness.[129]

Many disputes arise over the definition of an "equal" product. The owner and architect generally determine whether or not the substituted product is equal to the one named in the bidding documents. Whenever possible, a contractor should offer any substitutions prior to its bid for approval by the owner. After all the bids are submitted, a substitution request may become a battle between a general contractor or subcontractor seeking a lower-cost alternative and an owner or architect who may see the substitution as an inferior product or technique. In limited instances, an agency may specify an exact brand or "sole source" for the product or service.

The Public Contract Code also addresses subletting and subcontracting requirements,[130] which are intended to protect subcontractors and the public bidding process from unethical substitution or browbeating by the general contractor after submission and acceptance of the bid by the public agency. The Subletting and Subcontracting Fair Practices Act[131] includes provisions relating to bid shopping and bid peddling, listing of subcontractors in the bid, substitution, assignment and subletting of subcontractors, clerical errors in the listing of subcontractors, and many other important provisions.

Other provisions of the Public Contract Code relate to relief of bidders for certain mistakes,[132] requirements for the awarding of contracts,[133] contract sanctions for the employment of illegal aliens,[134] and even sanctions for out-of-state contractors from states that provide bidding penalties against nonresident (meaning California) contractors.[135]

§ 5.2.2 *Contracting by State Agencies*

Contracting by state agencies is governed by the State Contract Act;[136] however, the act is not applicable in every situation. For example, contracts for the purchase of certain materials and supplies by the Department of General Services are specifically excluded.[137] The eight provisions discussed below are of particular importance in the administration of contracts by state agencies. Other general provisions of lesser importance relating to state contracts are set forth in Public Contract Code §§ 10102—10110.

§ 5.2.2(a) *MBE/WBE/DVE*

Provisions aiding the interests of minority, women, and disabled veteran business enterprises are codified in Public Contract Code § 10115. The provisions once required contracts awarded by any state agency to provide participation goals of at least 15 percent for minority business enterprises, 5 percent for women business enterprises, and 3 percent for disabled veteran business enterprises. Currently, these have been held in violation of the equal protection clause of the California and U.S. Constitutions. In addition, California Proposition 209 has prohibited their use in State of California contracting.

Affirmative action procedures have in the recent past been the basis of many bid protests by unsuccessful bidders on public works projects. In the past, bidders were required to adhere to "good faith effort" requirements (generally consisting of advertising and writing letters to potential "disadvantaged" subcontractors) to avoid potential disqualification. Adherence to any fixed quota or percentage has been held to be an invalid application of these statutes.

Under prior law, a state agency was to consider the good faith efforts of the lowest responsible bidder in meeting minority, women, and disabled business enterprise goals.[138] Such good faith efforts and affirmative action programs have been highly controversial, and legal cases involving these programs have had mixed results before U.S. federal courts and the California Supreme Court.[139]

In a 1994 case involving Domar Electric, Inc., the court upheld a City of Los Angeles charter requirement that bidders make good faith efforts to comply with the city's **subcontractor outreach program**.[140] The program was designed to give minorities, women, and other groups an equal opportunity to participate in the performance of city contracts. In a second case involving Domar Electric, a contractor that submitted the lowest bid on a city public works project was not awarded the contract because it failed to document its compliance with the city's subcontractor outreach program.[141] The contractor challenged the decision to award the contract to another bidder on the grounds that the outreach program violated the city's charter, Public Contract Code § 2000 (award of a public contract to the lowest responsible bidder meeting minority participation requirements), and the **equal protection clause** of the U.S. Constitution, Amendment 14. The trial court denied the requested relief.[142] The court of appeal reversed the trial court's judgment, holding that the outreach program violated the city's charter, but the Supreme Court reversed the judgment of the court of appeal and remanded the matter.

On remand, the court of appeal affirmed the trial court's judgment. The city's outreach was judged to be not a "municipal affair" of competitive bidding and thus was subject to Public Contract Code § 2000. The court further held that the outreach program did not violate Contract Code § 2000, subd. (a)(2) (a public contract may be awarded to a bidder showing a good faith effort to obtain the participation of women and minorities, irrespective of the attainment of such participation), and it excluded the type of program described in § 2000, subd. (a)(1) (a bidder must have achieved a set number, percentage, or quota of participation or demonstrate a good faith [but unsuccessful] effort to encourage such participation.)

Under a U.S. Supreme Court decision, public entities that have not demonstrated past discrimination against minorities and women **cannot implement outreach programs** under Contract Code § 2000, subd. (a)(1), without violating the equal protection clause. For these entities, the programs allowed by Public Contract Code § 2000, subd. (a)(2) are the only option at the present time.[143]

In the Domar Electric case, the court ruled that even if a § 2000, subd. (a)(1), program had been constitutionally available, the city could still have elected to base its outreach efforts solely on subd. (a) (2). The court also held that the city's outreach program did not violate the equal protection clause of U.S. Constitution, Amendment 14, because the program did not require certain categories of subcontractors to be the beneficiaries of a prime contractor's outreach efforts or to be granted any preference.

As previously stated, the major purposes of using unfettered competitive bidding are to guard against favoritism, improvidence, extravagance, fraud, and corruption and to protect against insufficient competition so that the government gets the most work for the least money. Although mandatory set-asides and bid preferences work against this goal by narrowing the range of acceptable bidders solely on the basis of their particular classifications, requiring prime contractors to reach out to all types of subcontractors broadens the pool of participants in the bid process and thereby guards against the possibility of insufficient competition.[144]

In another recent case, a licensed engineer alleged that a county transportation authority's affirmative action program (as applied to the awarding of contracts) violated the right to equal protection under the law. The trial court found that the challenged program was unconstitutional. It entered an injunction barring further implementation of the program and awarded the plaintiff attorney fees.

The court of appeal reversed the judgment and the award of attorney fees and directed the trial court to enter a judgment in favor of the transportation authority on the basis that the plaintiff had no standing to pursue his action. First, the court of appeal held that the plaintiff lacked standing as an <u>individual</u> to challenge the program. To obtain a permanent injunction against further implementation of the program, the plaintiff had to show a specific invasion of a legally protected interest that was actual or imminent. The element of actual or imminent injury was lacking since the plaintiff failed to show that he was able and ready to bid on the transportation authority's contracts but discriminatory policies prevented him from doing so.

Second, the court held that the plaintiff lacked standing as a <u>taxpayer</u>[145] to challenge the program, since he was not a resident of the county and did not pay real property taxes in the county. The fact that plaintiff paid state income taxes was insufficient to confer standing upon him.

§ 5.2.2(b) Award to Lowest Responsible Bidder

All work on any state project must be performed under a contract awarded to the lowest responsible bidder.[146] *See* Chapter 9 for further discussion of this topic.

§ 5.2.2(c) Bid Advertisement

The Public Contract Code states that requests for bids must be advertised by public agencies and sets forth the requirements for such advertising.[147] *See* Chapter 8 for a more detailed discussion of this area.

§ 5.2.2(d) Bidding Requirements

Numerous requirements are applicable to those who bid on state public works contracts. Among the more important requirements are disclosure of financial statements indicating the "bidder's financial ability and experience in performing public works" projects,[148] submission of the sealed bids accompanied by bidder's security,[149] and withdrawal of bids prior to the time designated for opening of the bids.[150]

§ 5.2.2(e) Contract Award

The Public Contract Code makes provisions relating to the opening of bids publicly, awarding of the contracts and rejection of bids by public entities.[151] Provisions are also made relating to administration of contracts, including bond requirements,[152] damages for delay,[153] changes in plans and specifications,[154] and compliance with other agencies' procedures.[155]

§ 5.2.2(f) Resolution of Claims and Arbitration

The Public Contract Code provides for the resolution of contract claims, including arbitration, as the exclusive remedy for disputes involving State of California contracts disputes. Specific procedures must be followed to initiate arbitration. *See* Chapter 13 for further discussion of this area.[156]

§ 5.2.2(g) Changes and Extra Work

This aspect of public works contracting results in disputes between the involved parties. The provisions governing contract modifications (including changes and extra work provisions), performance, and payment must be carefully reviewed as they are important when dealing with or attempting to avoid potential claims.[157]

§ 5.2.2(h) University Rules

The University of California has competitive bidding requirements for projects exceeding $50,000.[158] The University of California generally takes the position that it is not bound by the provisions of the Public Contract Code pertaining to State of California contracts. It often refers to its status under the California Constitution as a separate branch of government, owing to issues of campus academic independence and freedom. However, the Public Contract Code does contain provisions relating specifically to California State University contracting.[159]

§ 5.2.3 Contracting by Local Agencies

The provisions governing contracting by local agencies (school districts, general law counties and cities and other special districts) are referred to collectively as the Local Agency Public Construction Act.[160] The provisions summarized below are of particular importance. Other provisions relating to specific local agencies are set forth in Contract §§ 20105—22300.

§ 5.2.3(a) School Districts

Contracts for school projects must be awarded through competitive bidding.[161] The bids must be sealed when submitted and accompanied by a form of bidder's security.[162] The Public Contract Code also contains other provisions that govern bidding and letting of contracts by school districts.[163]

§ 5.2.3(b) General Law Counties and Cities

A general county or city "has the powers expressly conferred by the state legislature."[164] Its power stems from the laws passed by the legislature; therefore, it has no power independent of the state legislature. Many provisions of the Public Contract Code govern public works contracts awarded by general law counties, including publication of advertisements for bids, award of contracts, modifications to the scope of work, rejection of bids, extra work, and method of payment.[165] Separate provisions apply to public works contracts awarded by counties with populations of less than 500,000.[166] The provisions for the majority of general law counties and cities are governed by the same sections of the code, except for special provisions that affect very large counties (generally pertaining only to Los Angeles County). Contracts awarded by general law cities are also subject to specific provisions contained in the Public Contract Code.[167]

§ 5.2.3(c) Transit, Utility, and Special Districts

Numerous sections of the Public Contract Code relate to various aspects of public works construction by specific transit, utility, and other districts.[168] A thorough investigation of each district's unique requirements is recommended.

§ 5.2.4 *Chartered Cities and Counties*

Unless a particular public agency is specifically stated in the Public Contract Code to be subject to its provisions, the Public Contract Code probably does not apply. Charter cities and counties, for example, are not subject to many provisions of the Public Contract Code.

A charter city or county is one that is self-governing and has formally adopted a city or county charter. The city or county is therefore generally subject only to the public works procurement provisions contained in its charter. As a rule, it has complete and total power over all its affairs.[169] Of course, all pertinent federal laws are enforceable in charter cities and counties.

It is well established that cities and general law cities are not subject to the same requirements for similar projects.[170] Further, the court has held that charter cities are not subject to the competitive bidding requirements of the Public Contract Code.[171]

In one case, a labor union sought to enjoin work being done by city employees on a city-owned pier on the grounds that state law and the city's charter required competitive bidding. The court held that the mode of contracting work by a charter city is a municipal rather than a statewide concern and that state bidding procedures did not apply.[172]

Before bidding on any public works project, a contractor should determine whether the public entity involved is a charter or general law entity. If it is a charter entity, the contractor should carefully read the entity's charter provisions regarding the letting of public works contracts.

§ 5.2.5 *Other Applicable California Codes*

Depending upon the public project and public entity contracting for the project, other California codes often apply to public works contracting, including the Agriculture Code, Government Code, Streets and Highways Code, Water Code, Education Code, and Public Utilities Code. Contractors should be familiar with applicable codes.

§ 5.3 CALIFORNIA PUBLIC RECORDS ACT

When public works disputes arise, public parties often seek information and documents from public entities through the Public Records Act.[173] The act, which is analogous to the federal Freedom of Information Act,[174] provides for the right of every person to inspect public records and receive copies.[175] "Public records" include writings that relate to the conduct of the public's business that are retained by any state or local agency.[176]

Certain records are exempt from disclosure, such as notes and interoffice memoranda, personnel records, medical records whose release would constitute an invasion of privacy, and confidential information.[177] However, if a public entity discloses a record that is otherwise exempt from disclosure, such action constitutes a waiver of the exemption by the public agency.[178]

The most significant exemption under the Public Records Act regarding disputes is the litigation privilege.[179] This privilege exempts from disclosure records pertaining to pending litigation to which the public agency is a party, or to claims made pursuant to Division 3.6 (commencing with § 810) of Title 1 of the Government Code, until such litigation or claim has been finally adjudicated or otherwise settled.[180] This provision is often used by public entities to withhold information. However, public entities must carefully analyze the provisions in this section so as not to subvert the purpose of the Public Records Act, which is to allow citizens access to the ordinary records of their government.

§ 5.4 FEDERAL PUBLIC LAW CONSIDERATIONS

A substantial number of federal construction projects in the state of California are directly performed by federal agencies. These include projects performed by the Department of the Navy in San Diego and San Francisco Bay areas, the U.S. Army Corps of Engineers with regard to a variety of ports and waterways throughout California, and the U.S. Bureau of Reclamation and the U.S. Army Corps of Engineers with regard to flood control and irrigation improvements, federal courthouses, congressional facilities, and other infrastructures.

The vast majority of public works contracts issued by California public agencies are not governed by federal contracting law. The major exceptions are federally funded mass transit (particularly rail transportation projects), flood control projects, highway improvements, airport projects, (especially those performed under FAA grants), and construction projects funded by locally administered federal grants.

The standard forms governing federal public works are set forth in the Federal Acquisition Regulations (FARS),[181] which are the primary regulations in use by all federal agencies for construction contract procurement. FARS sets forth bidding procedures and requires public contracts to be awarded to the lowest responsible and responsive bidders.

One important aspect to consider when dealing with a federal agency is that a "fair proportion" of federal contracts should be awarded to small businesses.[182] This requirement is similar to state contract minority and women business enterprise requirements,[183] discussed above. Generally, the U.S. Small Business Administration establishes the criteria used to determine whether a contractor qualifies as a small business.

Many federally instigated provisions are contained in the projects' construction contracts and bidding documents. The sources of many of these provisions are the grant agreement between the California public agency involved and the federal agency administering the grant and the rules and regulations associated with the federal grant and appropriations act for the funds. Government provisions are also included both in congressional legislation and federal regulations. Contractors and their attorneys must be highly familiar with the conditions of the granting agencies, including the substantive requirements for grant payments. Additionally, practitioners must have a working knowledge of the grant agencies procedures for protest bids, administration of disputes, and adjudication of legal disputes.

§ 5.5   Contacts with Public Officials

California attorneys generally have an ethical responsibility not to contact represented opposing parties.[184] However, the rules are different when it comes to public works projects, where the ultimate decision makers are elected public officials. Elected public officials are expected to communicate with and be responsive to members of the public, including taxpayers and vendors who do business with public agencies. Thus, despite the existence of city attorneys and county counsel, parties and their counsel, in disputes with public agencies regarding public works construction, regularly contact mayors, members of the city council, and county supervisors, as well as other elected officials.[185]

Contractors, therefore, have an advantage in certain situations that they would not have in the private sector (*e.g.* if a contractor's attorney directly contacted members of a board of directors or other representatives of corporations, he or she would be in violation of disciplinary rules). This matter is addressed often by city attorneys or county counsel in closed sessions, where public officials are discouraged from engaging in direct discussions with adverse parties during litigation.

Chapter 6

INSURANCE & BONDING

The Old Lassen Courthouse
Courtesy University of California Library, Davis California

Summary:
Risks inherent in public works contracts are outlined in this chapter. The various types of construction insurance coverage available to the involved parties are summarized. This chapter also discusses the two major forms of bonding (payment and materials bonds and performance bonds), the difference between bonding and insurance and surety litigation. Further, two legal cases are discussed that illustrate the complex subject of insurance coverage litigation. The Cates case is cited and discussed with regard to surety litigation.

§ 6.1 PROJECT RISKS

Many risks are inherent in the construction of new public works projects, and to the extent possible, those risks should be protected against with complete insurance coverage. The primary risks involve availability of the site, permitting and environmental approvals, project financing, insolvency of the general contractor, delay in the completion of construction, budget overruns, construction accidents, defects in the structure and catastrophic events. It is critical to note, however, that many of these risks are not insurable. Both the insurable and uninsurable risks are allocated among the involved entities by the project contracts or governing statutes or case law.

§ 6.2 CONSTRUCTION INSURANCE AND BONDING PRACTICES

Insurance and bonding is a major part of the public works process. Public agencies' design professionals, and construction firms must all address this area when becoming involved with any public works construction project. Consultation with an insurance specialist is highly recommended before entering into a public works contract.

§ 6.3 CONSTRUCTION INSURANCE

The following is a brief overview of the various types of coverage and policies generally available. It is important to note that the highly complex fabric of construction insurance policies and exclusions–along with insurance company marketing and claims practices, the impact of case law, and the dynamics of the litigation process–often does not meet the reasonable coverage expectations of design professionals, contractors, and public agency owners.

The major coverages for construction projects are divided into liability policies and property policies. Liability policies protect the insured against legal liability and defense costs for claims asserted by third parties for negligent injury to persons or property. Generally, there must be an occurrence, often thought of as an accident or unexpected consequence, that leads to actual financial damage.

The principal liability coverages are set forth in Commercial General Liability Policies (CGL) carried by virtually all parties to the construction process. There are many written exclusions in these policies, and whether they extend to products liability, completed operations, explosion and underground liability, environmental impairment, contractual liability, professional liability, workmanship, subsidence, ultra hazardous activities (such as blasting), and other potential losses, depends on the policy language and manner of issuance. As base contract insurance requirements are minimal, most construction firms also carry umbrella coverage.

There are two substantial dangers in professional liability policies that are typically issued to design professionals, environmental remediation firms, and certain other construction participants. These policies are typically written on a claims made basis. Thus, if a claim is not made during a specific policy year, the policy will not cover the loss, even if the loss or negligent acts occurred during the policy year. Also, these policies may contain wasting aggregate provisions, meaning that as defense funds are expended, the policy limits decrease by the amount of defense funds.

An important form of liability coverage is contained in Worker's Compensation and Employers Liability policies. While Worker's Compensation is really no fault insurance, the policy will cover specified loss amounts for injuries to workers that are incurred in the scope of their employment. Generally, Worker's Compensation serves as a bar against suing the employer in typical employee injury claims. Employer Liability insurance covered more esoteric claims by employers under various state statutes and theories of liability. Worker's Compensation is required for contractors operating in California.

The typical property policy covers loss, destruction or damage to property owned by the insured. There are also policies for equipment floaters, auto coverage, goods in transit, etc. A major form of policy carried by most owners is the Builder's Risk Policy. The typical insurance policies provided by general contractors and subcontractors on a particular project are set forth in Article 11 of the AIA A201 General Conditions document.[186]

Each of the participants in a public works project has its own set of coverages and exclusions. In fact, it is not uncommon for 50 to 100 policies to be involved in a major public works construction accident or dispute. Conflicts often arise between subcontractors' insurance provisions and eventually affect the owner because of the inconsistency among policies. In this regard, it is critical to evaluate the insurance program, and the resulting covered and retained risks with regard to these additional criteria: limits and deductibles, named insured status, additional insured status, waivers of subrogation, written indemnity agreements, and the quality and financial strength of the respective carriers, and self-insurance programs. One crucial issue is whether the policy is self-consuming or a wasting aggregate policy. For such a case, the defense costs reduce the available coverage amounts. Thus, a hard fought case may leave no policy limit for an adverse verdict. On rare occasions, insurance companies will attempt to issue policies to general contractors or others with these provisions which should be highly discouraged.

There is a tremendous distinction between a certificate of insurance, which states generally the type of policy that has been issued, and the policy itself. Only a review of the insurance policy, with its policy limits, deductibles, insurance declarations, named and additional insureds, and exclusions will yield the true nature of coverages afforded by the policy. Finally, it is much easier to forge or alter a certificate of insurance than create an entire fraudulent policy form. Certificate forgery is a common problem in the industry.

§ 6.4 INSURANCE COVERAGE LITIGATION

The litigation of insurance coverage claims is extremely complex, as it involves highly technical policies and mountains of ever-changing case law. Illustrative of the ebb and flow of these cases are <u>Cates Construction, Inc., et al. v. Talbot Partners</u> and <u>Glenfed Development Corp. v. Superior Court</u>, which are discussed below.

Extrinsic evidence of what is intended to be covered by a policy can include discovery of the insurance company's claim adjustment manuals and other internal documents. In the <u>Glenfed</u> case,[187] after an insured real estate developer's excess insurance carrier denied coverage of the insured's claims, the insured brought an action for declaratory relief and reformation, as well as damages for breach of contract and breach of the implied covenant of good faith and fair dealing. Reformation means the court interprets the contract using reformed or modified terms intended to effect the original intent of the parties. During discovery, the trial court denied the insured's motion to compel production of the insurer's claims manual, finding that the insured had failed to show good cause for its production.[188]

The court of appeal ordered the trial court to (1) void its order denying the insured's motion to compel production of the insurer's claims manual and (2) enter a new order granting the motion. Although a party who seeks to compel production of documents must show "good cause" where there is no privilege issue or claim of attorney work product, that burden is met simply by showing relevance.[189] Since claims manuals are admissible in coverage dispute litigation, it follows that they are discoverable. As for this manual's relevancy, the insurance code requires insurers to maintain guidelines for processing claims, and these guidelines are maintained in claims manuals.[190] Since virtually all policies detail the manner in which claims must be presented, the instruction manual for the insurer's employees was very likely to address such policy terms. Also, in this type of litigation, extrinsic evidence as to reasonable expectations of the insured may be admissible at trial. Even if it was inadmissible at trial, the claims manual could lead to the discovery of other, relevant evidence that was admissible.[191]

§ 6.5 BONDING

There are two major forms of bonds, those that 1) guarantee the payment of the general contractor's subcontractors (the so called payment and materials bond) and 2) those that guarantee the actual performance of the general contractor (performance bond). Unlike insurance policies, the bonding companies are not absorbing the contractor's risk of non-payment or performance, which remains with the contractor. However, in the event of insolvency or failure of performance of the contractor, the bonding company is obligated to complete the project and pay the subcontractors and materialman if the appropriate bonds have been written. The bonding company then pursues the contractor and its ownership for repayment, generally under corporate and personal indemnity agreements.

Dealing with contractor's bond sureties, the Second District Court of Appeal in <u>Federal Insurance Company v. Superior Court</u>, 60 CA 4 1370 (1998), found that a subcontractor's claim on a payment bond must be stayed by the court, along with the subcontractor's claim against the general contractor, pending the outcome of the general contractor/subcontractor arbitration proceeding and pursuant to the arbitration provisions found in the subcontractor/contractor contract.

Bonds also differ from insurance policies when a bonding company becomes insolvent. When an admitted insurance carrier becomes insolvent, the State of California Insurance Guarantee Fund provides certain financial protections to policy holders. However, there is no State of California guarantee fund for sureties or bonding companies. Furthermore, many bonding companies respond to claims by simply reiterating the claim and contract positions of the contractor, meaning the bond becomes little more than a guarantee of any ultimate judgment against the contractor for non-performance or non-payment. The track record of sureties varies greatly. Thus, the quality and financial strength of the bonding companies is a primary issue for owners, subcontractors, and material vendors on California projects.

§ 6.6 SURETY LITIGATION

For many years, it was not clear whether claimants could sue a surety for bad faith. The issue had been decided in the negative for general insurance policies, where only the insured itself was eligible to bring an action for bad faith against an insurer. A bad faith action had special allure since it allowed for punitive damages as well as recovery on actual losses. The question was whether, under a surety bond, the principal (normally the general contractor) or the claimants (arguably the persons the bond was intended to protect) were eligible to bring a bad faith lawsuit. This question was largely answered in the Cates case. (See author's note at the bottom of page 73.)

In Cates, a commercial surety company and a contractor, as the surety's principal, brought an action against a developer and its lender alleging breach of the construction contract. The claimants sought foreclosure on a mechanic's lien and declaratory relief, which, in this case, is a rapid judicial determination of insurance contract issues, such as whether an obligation to defend exists, the extent of coverage, and the meaning of excuses and extensions of policy terms. The developer cross-complained against the contractor for breach of the construction contract and against the surety for recovery under the performance bond, breach of the performance and labor and materials payment bonds, and breach of the implied covenant of good faith and fair dealing. The lender also cross-complained against the surety for breach of the bonds. The trial court awarded compensatory damages to the developer and the lender, and a jury awarded the developer $28 million in punitive damages.[192]

The court of appeal modified the judgment to reduce the amount of punitive damages to be $15 million, remanded the matter back to the trial court for a recalculation of prejudgment interest on the awards to the developer and its lender, and affirmed the judgment in all other respects. Prejudgment interest is interest awarded in a lawsuit based upon a fixed contract sum or other "liquidated" amount that has become due. It is intended to put the recovering party in the same position economically had the debt been paid. A liquidated amount is a sum that can be ascertained without a lengthy factual hearing, such as the payment on a note or undisputed invoice for goods.

The court of appeal held that the developer was not prevented from bringing a cause of action for breach of the implied covenant of good faith and fair dealing.[193] Surety bonds are insurance, and the same implied covenant of good faith and fair dealing applicable to insurance contracts generally applies to surety bonds. The court also held that the developer was entitled to tort damages. The rule that permits tort damages for breach of the implied covenant of good faith in insurance contracts is based on the unique characteristics of insurance, and that rule was found to apply to the surety insurance in this case. Furthermore, the court stated that the record contained sufficient evidence to support the jury's findings of malice and oppression so as to support an award of punitive damages. Thus, punitive damages were properly awarded against the surety, although federal due process requirements mandated a reduction of the amount awarded.

An award of $15 million was found to be commensurate with the surety's acts and its wealth, the injury, and the state's interest in good faith performance of insurance contracts. Lastly, the court of appeal held that the measure of damages applied by the trial court was correct.[194]

> (**Author's Note!!!** At press time, the California Supreme Court largely reversed the Court of Appeal decision in <u>Cates</u>. Readers are encouraged to see the full published decision when available.)

Chapter 7

CONTRACTOR LICENSING LAW

The Old Modoc County Courthouse, Alturas
Courtesy University of California Library, Davis California

Summary:
An overview of the California Contractor's State License Law is presented (Business & Professions Code Sections 7000-7173), discussing requirements, classifications of licenses and which license is necessary for the different areas of the construction industry, unlicensed contractors, and exemptions from the law. The special requirements that apply to joint venture licenses are discussed. In addition, the author discusses the perpetual problem of licensing joint ventures and other temporary business entities citing legal cases which illustrate the effects of noncompliance with licensing laws.

§ 7.1 OVERVIEW OF LICENSING LAW

The statutory provisions governing the licensing of contractors in California are contained in Bus. & Prof. Code §§ 7000—7173. This comprehensive body of law sets forth the requirements for obtaining a construction license, the penalties for performing work without a license, and the various licensing classifications available.

The purpose of the California licensing law is to protect the public from incompetence and dishonesty in those who provide building and construction services[195] and to guard the public against unskilled workmanship and deception.[196]

The Contractor's State License Board is the agency responsible for administering the license law and is included within the Department of Consumer Affairs of the State of California. The responsibilities of the Board include reviewing and investigating complaints made against contractors and administering disciplinary action against contractors found to have violated any aspect of the licensing provisions.

§ 7.2 WHO NEEDS A LICENSE?

A contractor (which includes a builder, subcontractor, or specialty contractor) is defined by Business and Professional Code § 7026 as one who either undertakes or conveys the authority to undertake the construction, alteration, repair, improvement, or demolition of any building, road, or other structure. Anyone engaging in the above activities is required to possess a valid California state contractor's license.

Oftentimes, an individual does not construct, alter or repair an entire structure, but performs only a small fraction of work on a building. California case law indicates that when a small portion of work technically requires a contractor's license but substantially all of the work does not, failure to obtain a license is not fatal, and the contractor is likely to prevail on its efforts to collect payment.[197]

On the other hand, the court has found that in some cases a valid license is required to perform only a portion of a project. In one case, an individual who assisted a drywall contractor and framing contractor, and who was to be paid for labor on a square-foot basis and for materials on a cost-reimbursement basis, was required to possess a valid contractor's license.[198] Had the individual worked simply for wages and had the materials been provided by the general contractor, full payment would probably have been compelled by the court. The court also held that a valid contractor's license was required by an individual who provided a loader and trucks and removed dirt from one site and transported it to another.[199] Lastly, the court required a person who furnished topsoil and finished grading a site to possess a valid contractor's license.[200]

As you can see, there is a fine line between when a license is required and when a license may not be required. Public agencies and contractors should contact the State License Board to determine whether a license may be required for the particular types of work they plan to undertake.

§ 7.3 License Classification/Requirements for Public Contracts

Two provisions of the Contract Code relate to the licensing classification and requirements for bidding on a public project. The first is contained within the administrative provisions and requires all public entities to specify the license classification the selected contractor must possess at the time the public works contract is awarded.[201] The public entity must include the required license classification on any plans prepared by the public entity, as well as all invitations to bid.[202] This provision applies to only those contractors who have a direct contractual relationship with the public entity and not those who subcontract with the general contractor.[203]

The second provision relates to contracting by state agencies and requires the contractor to possess a valid contractor's license if awarded a state contract involving federal funds.[204] The state agency must verify that the contractor awarded the project possesses the appropriate classification necessary to perform the work.[205]

§ 7.4 Which License Is Necessary?

Contained within the statutory provisions governing the licensing of contractors in the state of California are the various classifications assigned to different areas of the construction industry.[206]

Three main classifications are prescribed by statute: Class A, Class

B, and Class C. Class A encompasses general engineering contractors,[207] Class B refers to general building contractors,[208] and Class C refers to all other specialty contractors outside the general building classification,[209] such as electrical contractor (C10), plumbing contractor (C36), and swimming pool contractor (C53), to name but a few. The licensing board administers individual examinations for the various classifications, as well as trades or crafts within the classifications, then it qualifies applicants for approval if they are successful on the examinations.[210]

The Class A general engineering contractor is defined by the Contract Code as one involved with fixed works requiring specialized engineering knowledge and skill, including items such as flood control structures, dams, harbors, shipyards, railroads, highways and streets, and airports.[211]

The Class B general building contractor is one whose principal business is building a structure for the "support, shelter, and enclosure of persons, animals, chattels or movable property of any kind..."[212] In order for the Class B license to be applicable, the construction of the building described above must involve more than two unrelated trades or crafts.[213] An individual performing two or fewer trades must possess a valid specialty license, as discussed below.

The Class C specialty contractor is one who performs work requiring specific skills or knowledge in the area of a specialized building trade or craft.[214] A specialty contractor may perform specialty work for which it does not possess a license, so long as that work is incidental and supplemental to the work for which the contractor is licensed. A case illustrating this point involved a plumbing contractor who was permitted to perform fire protection work without a fire protection license owing to the "incidental nature of fire protection work in general."[215]

Any business licensed to perform contracting work in the state of California must currently employ at least one individual who meets all the criteria for licensure within the applicable classification.[216] This individual is referred to as the Responsible Managing Employee (RME) or Responsible Managing Officer (RMO). Extensions of time may be granted in certain circumstances. A business temporarily without an RME or RMO must fill the position with another qualifying individual within ninety days or its license will automatically be suspended.[217]

Special requirements apply to joint venture licenses. Each member (individual, corporation, or partnership) of the joint venture is required to individually possess a valid contractor's license.[218] However, only one member of the joint venture is required to be licensed in the classification in which the joint venture is licensed.[219] The loss of any member's license or the departure of any member from the joint venture will result in the loss of the joint venture's license.[220] Joint ventures may bid on work without a license, but must obtain the applicable license classification prior to being awarded a contract.[221] Other licensable contractors may not bid on work without a license, although the statute is somewhat ambiguous after its 1987 revision.

§ 7.5 UNLICENSED CONTRACTORS

Many people claim to be licensed contractors when, in fact, they are not licensed.

The consequence of unlicensed work is generally the lack of any right to payment for work performed. Bus. & Prof. Code § 7031(a) prevents any unlicensed individual from recovery for the performance on any contract for which a valid contractor's license is required, regardless of the merits of the unlicensed contractor's claim.[222] In a California Supreme Court case, the court concluded that the § 7031 bar against suits by unlicensed contractors applies even when the owner fraudulently and knowingly entices an unlicensed contractor to enter into a contract.[223] In this case, an out-of-state contractor was barred from suing for fraud. The court stated, "[R]egardless of the equities, § 7031 bars all actions, however, they are characterized, which effectively seek `compensation' for illegal unlicensed contract work."[224] Thus, an unlicensed contractor cannot recover either for the agreed-upon contract price or for the reasonable value of labor and materials.[225]

However, § 7031 allows the courts to determine there has been substantial compliance under this section if the unlicensed contractor can prove he or she was properly licensed just prior to performance under the contract at issue and was unaware he or she did not possess a valid license when the work was performed.[226] One California case that demonstrates the uncertainty associated with § 7031(d) involved a question of whether a corporate contractor's president, who was personally licensed, was the RMO of the corporation, thereby making the corporation licensed under the substantial performance test.[227] Generally, substantial performance is defined as conformance with all the substantive aspects of the statute, giving the consumers essentially the same degree of protection as had the contractor been fully licensed.

Other exceptions to strict compliance with § 7031 have been allowed by federal courts, as well as by California courts. One such exception is that an unlicensed contractor need not refund monies paid on a contract for which a valid contractor's license is required.[228] Another exception permits an unlicensed contractor to sue subcontractors for defective work.[229] Lastly, a California case concluded that an unlicensed contractor may be able to apply an unpaid contract balance as a setoff in a lawsuit brought by an owner.[230]

The prohibition against an unlicensed individual recovering contract or claims sums also applies to a party that obtains an assignment of the claim through factoring the receivable or purchasing the claim. In Construction Financial v. Perlite Plastering Co.,[231] the trial court dismissed a subcontractor's action for breach of contract and related causes of action against two construction companies and an insurer on the grounds that the subcontractor did not show substantial compliance with the Contractors' State License Law.[232]

The court of appeal affirmed, holding that substantial evidence supported the trial court's dismissal of the action. The trial court's finding that the subcontractor's negligence caused it not to have a valid license was enough to support the judgment, since the 1991 version of Bus. & Prof. Code § 7031, subd. (d) (applicable to this action since it was effective on December 20, 1993), exempted from licensure requirements only those contractors whose unlicensed status was the result of circumstances beyond their control. Furthermore, although the defendant general contractor was aware of the plaintiff's licensure status, and the plaintiff relied upon the defendant's advice in connection with its license, Business and Professional Code § 7031 applied.

§ 7.6 Exemptions from the License Law

Numerous exemptions from the Contractors' State License Law exist.[233] One exemption is for minor or inconsequential projects for which labor and materials do not amount to more than $300 in the aggregate.[234] This exemption also applies to material suppliers.[235] However, a fine line is drawn when applying this particular exemption. In one case, California courts stated a license was required of a prefabricated-pool installer whose work required significant excavation and other work.[236] In another case, a license was not required of a prefabricated-restroom manufacturer whose employees assemble components and bolt the unit to a foundation.[237]

Another important exemption applies to "owner/builders."[238] This exemption typically applies when the owner performs the work on his or her own or uses his or her own employees to do the work.[239] Lastly, an exemption applies to architects and engineers performing solely within their professional capacities.[240]

§ 7.7 EFFECTS OF FAILURE TO PROPERLY LICENSE ENTITIES

One area of perpetual problems is the licensing of joint ventures and other temporary business entities and relationships. In general, a lack of licensing compliance will result in nonpayment, as well as other calamities.

For example, in Ranchwood Communities Limited Partnership v. Jim Beat Construction Co.,[241] the homeowner's associations of two separate condominium projects brought construction defect actions against the developers who administered the projects as unlicensed general contractors. The defendants cross-complained against numerous subcontractors on the projects for equitable and implied contractual indemnity, contribution, negligence, and certain contract-based theories. The trial court granted summary judgments for the subcontractors and dismissed the cross-complaints, finding them barred by Bus. & Prof. Code § 7031 (barring actions brought by unlicensed contractors for compensation for work performed).[242]

The court of appeal reversed the summary judgments and remanded the case for further proceedings because, in their capacity as developers, the defendants were not subject to a bar to their pursuit of recovery on tort theories of indemnity and contribution by reason of their lack of contractors' licenses.

The court held that the defendants did not show substantial compliance with the licensing statute or exemption from licensing requirements because they were owner/builders within the meaning of Business and Professional Code § 7044. Neither the fact that an owner/lender of one of the contractors obtained a license for the last year of the seven-year construction period nor the contractors' hiring of licensed subcontractors or a licensed general contractor as manager raised triable issues to show substantial compliance.

Furthermore, although Business and Professional Code § 7044 was amended in 1989 (following completion of the above projects), the legislature's intent was to clarify existing law.[243] Hence, the statute was properly applied retroactively to exclude these contractors from the statute's owner/builder exemption. The court further held that the contract-based claims (for express indemnity, breach of contract and warranties, and declaratory relief) were barred by the licensing requirements of Business and Professional Code § 7031.

The tort-based cross-claims (for equitable indemnity, implied contractual and total indemnity, and contribution) were not barred by Business and Professional Code § 7031, since the primary relief sought was not compensation for work performed but rather equitable indemnification for the damages for which the defendants were strictly liable as developers of defective construction projects. Similarly, negligence claims against the subcontractors were outside the scope of the contractual claims, and thus were not barred by the licensing requirements. However, under Code of Civ. Proc. § 877, subd. (a), to the extent that any subcontractors paid negligence damages to the homeowners, the developer/contractor would be entitled to appropriate credit.[244]

§ 7.8 Conclusion

California's Contractors' State License Law, although at times cumbersome, is intended to preserve the quality of workmanship every owner is entitled to when contracting with one who possesses superior knowledge in an area of construction. It is interesting that many large industrial states, such as New Jersey, do not feel a need to license contractors. In that light, sophisticated owners based their hiring decisions on the experience, skill, and references of the proposing contractor. The lesson is that the mere possession of a contractor's license does not guarantee competency in the specific project to be undertaken. This is an important point for consideration later, when the bidding process (Chapter 8) and bid protests are described. Ultimately, the contracting public agency and contracting community is responsible for ensuring that buildings and other structures conform to the required standards within the industry, such that the soundness, safety, and code compliance of structures in the community are not compromised.

CHAPTER 8

THE BIDDING PROCESS

Nevada City Courthouse
Courtesy University of California Library, Davis California

Summary:

The competitive bidding requirements for public works projects are discussed in this chapter. "Responsive" and "responsible" bidders are defined. Other provisions are outlined addressing various aspects of the bidding process, including solicitation, submission, and withdrawal of bids; bid mistakes, the Subletting and Subcontracting Fair Practices Act; bid evaluation, prevailing wages; circumstances under which the courts permit an agency to bypass competitive bidding, as well as the administrative and legal challenges of bid protests by unsuccessful bidders. Supporting case law is cited and discussed. Specialized equipment requirements are addressed in addition to information that must be supplied by the public agency to the bidders.

§ 8.1 Competitive Bidding Requirements

Public works contracts are subject to numerous competitive bidding requirements, which are set forth in the Contract Code. The public works bidding process generally involves the submittal of sealed bids by all bidders on a specific date and to a specific place prior to an ironclad time deadline. The bids are then opened and read, and typically the lowest bidder is awarded the contract and becomes the general contractor.

Competitive bidding requirements serve several important purposes. As previously discussed, bidding laws exist to protect the public from misuse or waste of public funds, provide all qualified bidders with a fair opportunity to enter the bidding process, stimulate competition in a manner conducive to sound fiscal practices, and eliminate favoritism, fraud, corruption, and abuse of discretion in the awarding of public contracts.[245]

However, the Contract Code provisions are narrowly construed so, unless a particular public entity is specifically subject to its provision, the Contract Code will not apply. For example, several California courts have held that <u>charter</u> cities are not subject to the Contract Code competitive bidding provisions.[246]

The general rules of contract law are applicable to the competitive bidding process. Bids are considered irrevocable offers or options.[247] Public agencies generally take the position that competitive bidding requirements exist for the benefit of the public and were not established to protect individual bidders.[248]

Typically, if the cost of a public works project exceeds a certain dollar amount set forth in the applicable Contract Code provision, the contract <u>must</u> be awarded through competitive bidding. Dollar amount thresholds for competitive bidding range from $10,000 to $75,000, depending on the type of transaction or type of purchase involved. Projects costing less than the threshold amount may be subject to sole source or negotiated contracts in the best interest of the awarding public entity.[249] A public works contract is usually awarded to the lowest bidder because the low price is presumed to be the fairest price to the public.

However, several statutory exceptions exist to the competitive bidding requirements for public works contracts. For example, Contract Code § 10340(b)(1) provides an exception where a contract is necessary for public health, safety, or welfare, or for the protection of government property. Other California statutes provide exceptions for certain types of architectural/engineering contracts.[250] Emergency situations are also typically exempted. In addition, some flexibility is required in situations where the original contractor is being terminated for cause or convenience, and the bonding company has not supplied a substitute contractor.

Mass transit has many specialized equipment requirements, and a limited number of suppliers for certain system components. Public Utility Code § 130238 sets forth exceptions to the competitive bidding requirements for public works projects involving specialized rail transit equipment and electronic equipment that are not available in substantial quantities to the general public. "Specialized equipment" includes rail cars, computer equipment, telecommunications and microwave equipment, fare collection systems, and other types of electronic equipment.

However, this exception <u>does not</u> apply to any products, including "specialized equipment," that are, essentially, off-the-shelf, that is available in substantial quantities to the general public. When two-thirds of the awarding agency determines by vote that a particular type of equipment can be properly classified as "specialized" under Public Utility Code § 130238, the agency is not required to award the contract to the lowest bidder. In addition to price, an agency may consider factors such as vendor financing, performance reliability, standardization, life-cycle costs, delivery timetables, support logistics, fitness of purchase, and manufacturer's warranties.

California courts have also recognized that exceptions may apply to the competitive bidding requirements in other situations.[251] Generally, the courts will permit the awarding agency to bypass competitive bidding when it would be "undesirable or impossible to advertise for bids for particular work."[252]

<u>Construction Industry Force Account Council v. Amador Water Agency</u>. 99 C.D.O.S. 3048, (1999). A local water agency, Amador, installed a water pipeline with its own personnel. The Construction Industry Force Council challenged the agency's right to complete the project without

soliciting bids from outside contractors first. The council argued that Public Contract Code Section 21451 prohibits an agency from using its own employees on a project that costs more than $12,500 (Amador spent approximately $133,000).

The trial court held that Section 24151 applies when an agency chooses to contract for a project over $12,500, but does force an agency to contract for such a project.

The Court of Appeal affirmed, holding that the section is ambiguous in regard to a monetary limit for "force accounts," and that because the Legislature has taken an "ad hoc" approach to granting public agencies authority regarding outside bids, it would be inappropriate to place such limits on agencies themselves.

Any public works contract that is excepted from the competitive bidding process must be advertised and may be challenged by any company that believes it can do the work at a lower price.[253]

One last note in this area is that when a contract is subject to competitive bidding requirements and has been executed without compliance, the courts have concluded the contract is void and unenforceable.[254]

§ 8.2 Bid "Responsiveness"

Bids are often rejected as "non-responsive" for highly technical reasons. Here are just a few examples of the kinds of situations where bids have been rejected for apparently minor reasons:

- The bid submission envelope failed to properly identify the project in question, even though the public agency at that time had no other proposals out for bid.
- The bidder delivered its bid bond one minute after the opening of the bids began.
- The bidder failed to fill in one line item in the bid package, even though the package contained numerous pages of documents.
- The bid specifications required that certain corporate officers were to sign the bid proposal. The officers were not available, so some one other than a specified corporate officer signed the bid proposal.
- The bidder submitted a proposal that acknowledged only twelve of the fourteen addenda presented in the bid package.

Usually, a public entity will expressly reserve in the bidding documents the right to reject any or all bids.[255]

The public entity will generally attempt to ensure the bidding process is fair and objective by insisting that all bidders compete on a level playing field. Therefore, forms are used so that all bids are identical in content except for price. To maintain fairness in the bidding process, the public entity must reject any bid that is not "responsive." A bid is considered responsive "if it promises to do what the bidding instructions demand."[256]

Guidelines have been developed by the courts for agencies considering whether to accept the lowest bid. Considering these factors is important as automatic rejection will result in substantial disruption of the bidding process and higher expense for the public entity. These guidelines are discussed below.

§ 8.2.1 "Responsiveness" Defined

A "responsive" bid is one that is in strict and full accordance with all material terms of the bid package.[257] For example, the bidder has used the correct bid forms, has fully completed all questionnaires, has submitted all requisite enclosures, and has provided a proper bid bond when security is required. Any material variations will place the bidder at risk of being rejected by the public entity as non-responsive.

Material terms include (1) terms that could affect price, quantity, and quality or delivery and (2) terms that are clearly identified by the public entity and that must be complied with at the risk of bid rejection. For example, failing to fill in all of the blanks or failing to submit all required attachments may be the basis for characterizing the bid as non-responsive.

One test often used to determine whether a bid fails to materially comply with the bidding documents is whether the failure to comply gives the bidder a substantial economic advantage or benefit not enjoyed by other bidders.[258]

§ 8.2.2 Immaterial Variances May Be Waived

Although full compliance with each provision of a bid package is the best way for a contractor to ensure that its bid is responsive, an immaterial requirement may be waived by the public entity without prejudicing unsuccessful bidders.[259] The failure to comply with an immaterial provision is called a "minor informality." These may include:

- failure to meet procedural requirements
- failure to meet substantive requirements that do not strictly comply with the bidding documents but that satisfactorily meet such requirements
- failure to meet requirements calling for information that relates only to independently verifiable facts regarding the bidder and do not relate to the bidder's ability or promise to perform the contract
- minor clerical errors

Minor informalities may also be dismissed if they affect the bid in a trivial or negligible manner. But although a "minor variance" in bid responsiveness may be the excuse, any deviation from the requirements of the bid package, no matter how small or seemingly insignificant, puts a bid at risk for being rejected due to non-responsiveness. For this reason, a bidder may find it useful to prepare a checklist for all bid requirements and submittals and to produce a schedule for obtaining the required items.

The case of <u>Ghilotti Const. Co. v. City of Richmond</u>[260] is an example of a low responsible bidder being awarded a contract even after failing to adhere to a fairly important bid specification. In <u>Ghilotti</u>, a city awarded a contract for a road construction project to the lowest bidder, even though the low bid deviated by a margin of 5.5 percent from contract specifications that limited subcontracting to 50 percent of the total bid. The trial court denied the second lowest bidder's petition for a writ of mandate or prohibition to prevent the city from contracting with the low bidder.[261]

The court of appeal affirmed, holding that the trial court properly denied the second lowest bidder's writ petition since the city had correctly concluded that the low bid's deviation from the contract specifications was inconsequential. The plaintiff's counsel conceded that there was no evidence showing that the low bidder would have submitted a higher bid had it complied with the specification restricting the use of subcontractors. Furthermore, the plaintiff failed to show that the low bidder had an unfair competitive advantage since the low bidder could comply with the subcontracting limitation without changing the amount of its bid by purchasing some materials directly instead of through subcontractors. The court also held that the city's award to the low bidder did not violate public policy since there was no evidence of favoritism toward the low bidder, corruption, fraud, extravagance, or uncompetitive bidding practices.

§ 8.3 BIDDER RESPONSIBILITY

§ 8.3(a) *"Responsibility" Defined.*

A responsive bid may be rejected if the public entity determines the bidding company is not "responsible." A bidder is not responsible if it is not inherently capable of performing a contract as promised.[262] This is an important area for public entities since the contractor will argue that the performance bond is ample protection for the public entity and that the license held by the bidder is sufficient evidence of competency. The following are a few of the major public works provisions that address the topic of bidder responsibility.

Contract Code § 10162 provides that a state agency may reject any bidder that has previously been "disqualified, removed, or otherwise prevented from bidding on, or completing a federal, state or local government project because of a violation of law or a safety regulation." Contract Code § 10303, relating to state agencies, permits rejection of a bidder for 90 to 360 days where the bidder's performance on prior state contracts "has demonstrated a lack of reliability in complying with and completing such previously awarded contracts." Contract Code § 10285.1 permits suspension of a bidder from public works contracts for up to three years where the contractor or any partner, member, officer, director, responsible managing officer, or responsible managing employee of the company has been convicted of fraud, bribery, collusion, conspiracy, or other violation of any state of federal antitrust law in connection with bidding on any public works contract.

A bidder may be able to satisfy the "responsibility" requirement through a pre-qualification process. For example, the State General Services Administration has pre-qualification programs for a variety of work categories.

§ 8.3(b) *Standard of Review*

Most public entities are required by statute, code, or city charter to award contracts through competitive bidding to the "lowest responsible bidder." Often the second or third lowest bidder on a project will complain that the public entity has erred in determining that the low bidder was "responsible." Though public agencies are given broad discretion when awarding public works contracts, courts will overturn a contract award decision if the public entity is judged to have acted arbitrarily or capriciously.[263]

California courts have held that when a statute requires a public works contract to be awarded to the lowest responsible bidder, it must be awarded to the lowest bidder unless that bidder is found to be not responsible, *i.e.,* not qualified to perform the particular work.[264] In this context, "responsible" refers not only to the attribute of trustworthiness but also to the quality, fitness, and capacity of the bidder to perform the proposed agreement satisfactorily.[265]

Although public entities have discretion in determining which bidders are responsible, the agency may not choose the superior bidder from a field of qualified bidders. If the agency determines that more than one bidder is responsible, it may not award the a contract on the basis of "relative superiority" or "superior technical ability." Making a determination on such a basis ignores the fact there are several contractors able to perform the work and thrusts the public entity into the dubious process of assessing on the relative strength of the bidders' qualifications. Under these circumstances, the public agency is expected to award the contract to the lowest bidder of the qualified group.[266]

The following are two examples of cases where a bidder was <u>not</u> considered to be responsible.

In <u>Raymond v. Fresno City Unified School Dist.</u>,[267] the Board of Education determined that the low bidder was not responsible because of numerous complaints and poor workmanship by the contractor on a prior school project. The appellate court affirmed the award to the second lowest bidder, finding that the Board of Education had not abused its discretion in determining that the plaintiff contractor's bid was not the "offer which best responded in quality, fitness, and capacity to the particular requirement of the proposed work."

In a second case, <u>R. & A. Vending Services, Inc. v. City of Los Angeles</u>,[268] the lowest bidder was not entitled to the contract because he had a reputation for poor performance on similar projects.

§ 8.3(c) Notice & Opportunity to be Heard for Unsuccessful Bidders

Prior to rejecting the lowest bidder on the basis of non-responsibility, the awarding agency must notify the bidder of the evidence supporting its findings and afford the bidder an opportunity to rebut this evidence and demonstrate that it is qualified to perform the work. It is not necessary, however, for the public agency to conduct a quasi-judicial hearing prior to rejecting the low bidder.[269]

§ 8.4 Solicitation of Bids

A public agency must publish a notice inviting bids for each project, which is essentially an advertisement soliciting the submission of formal bids by prospective bidders. The circulation requirements of such notices are defined by statute.[270]

The contents of the public notice are also defined by statute. The notice must include information such as the time and place for receiving and opening bids and a description of the work to be performed.[271] Other information included in the public notice and associated bid package is outlined below.

§ 8.4.1 *Pre-qualification*

Bidders often are asked to pre-qualify before submitting a major bid to a public entity. If pre-qualification is required, the criteria should be provided by the public entity prior to the invitation to bid.

The subject of pre-qualification of contractors is somewhat controversial. The traditional view of the general contracting community and its sureties was that as long as a contractor was properly licensed, could provide a surety bond, and was licensed to do business in California, the contractor should be allowed to bid on any project within the scope of its qualifications. The contrary view is that the public entity has the responsibility for assuring that contractors bidding on work are responsible not only for the work they performed in the past but also for the size, scope, and scale of the project on which they are currently bidding.

Attempts have been made in the California legislature to codify what is considered responsible and to provide pre-qualification procedures, but these efforts have been unsuccessful. On major projects, public entities often include in bidding materials their own questionnaires to draw out the qualifications, financial strength and experience of contractors so the public entities can do an adequate and comprehensive job of determining the responsibility of the contractors.

In pre-qualification, contractors are asked to submit all information pertinent to the determination of the responsibility several weeks (or months) before the bid date. The public agency can review the prior experience of each contractor, verify its references on similar work, and cross-check issues such as safety records and experience modifiers on multi-state workers' compensation ratings to determine if the contractor is, in fact, qualified to do the job. One favorable aspect of this approach is a contractor that is deemed to have insufficient experience to bid on a job is apprised of the fact well in advance of the bid deadline so it will not spend the time to estimate and bid the project unnecessarily. On the other hand, under the City of Inglewood,[272] a contractor that is denied an opportunity to bid would have a due process right to be heard and state its qualifications.

Under Contract Code § 10160 — § 10164, prospective bidders may be required to disclose items such as financial information and past safety records prior to the award of a contract. Typically, this information is presented on a questionnaire that is included in the bid package.[273] A detailed sample questionnaire is attached as Appendix A.

§ 8.4.2 *Licensing Requirements*

The Contractor's State Licensing Law[274] requires a license for any person or entity that constructs, alters, repairs, wrecks, demolishes, or improves any building. The purpose of the license requirement is "to protect the public from incompetence and dishonesty in those who provide building and construction services."[275] The licensing law is discussed in more detail in Chapter 7.

Any contractor submitting a bid to a public agency is required to possess a valid license. If a contract is executed between a public entity and an unlicensed person acting in the capacity of a contractor, the contract will be void with certain exceptions.[276] Minor or inconsequential projects are exempt from the licensing laws, as well as any person furnishing materials or supplies for a project.[277]

M & B Construction v. Yuba County Water Agency. 68 Cal. App 4th 1353, (1999). The Yuba County Water Agency requested bids from contractors with class "A" licenses. M & B Construction submitted the lowest bid, but was not class "A" licensed, so its bid was rejected.

M & B Construction filed suit against the water agency, claiming that its decision was based on favoritism and bias. The trial court agreed, mandating that all contractors licensed to perform the work in question be allowed to submit bids.

The court of appeal reversed, holding that the water agency had the right to require class "A" licensing for its project, because the agency's decision affected only the category of licensee (as opposed to who may actually be licensed), and related only to dealing between the agency and contractors, not to contractors and third parties.

§ 8.4.3 *Information to Be Supplied to Bidders*

A bid package is supplied to all prospective bidders responding to a public notice. The package typically contains a standard proposal form that must be completed by a bidder for submittal to the public entity.[278] The package also typically requires the bidder to supply substantial other information as outlined below.

The public entity provides general instructions to bidders regarding time, place, and date of submission; delivery requirements (sealed bid requirement); and opening of bids. In addition, specifications, which must be sufficiently detailed, definite, and precise, are provided for bidding.[279]

The bid specifications may provide for a designated material, product, or thing to be used in the construction of the project. The material or product specification must list at least two brand names or trade names of comparable quality and must be followed by the words "or equal" so bidders can propose a product substitution equal to the design specifications. This is termed an "or equal" clause.[280]

If bids will be subject to review based upon a preference statute (giving preference to domestic or local contractors and material suppliers), the bid specifications should refer to the preference.

The specifications must set forth any minority and disability requirements. In addition, the specifications should set forth bond and security requirements, if applicable, or alternatives to bonds such as letters of credit or certificates of deposits. Prevailing wage rate requirements, as well as workers compensation insurance and other insurance requirements, should also be included in the bid specifications.

§ 8.5 BID SUBMISSION

Before submitting its bid proposal, a bidder should carefully review all submittals to confirm all bid requirements have been satisfied.

Delivery requirements must be met as well. The bid must be delivered on time to the exact location listed in the bid package. Under most statutory, code, and charter provisions, the public entity cannot receive any late bids.[281]

The bid should also be sealed to ensure fairness in the review process. An unsealed bid may be deemed non-responsive for failing to meet the "sealed bid" requirement.[282]

Finally, usually a bid for public works contracts must include a bid security, either in the form of cash, a cashier's check, a certified check, or a bid bond issued by an approved surety. The statutory minimum for a bidder's security is 10 percent of the bid amount.[283] If the bidder is required to provide a performance bond, the bidder may wish to use a bid bond as security because a surety will rarely issue a bid bond without also issuing a performance bond.

When a bidder's security is required, failure to provide such security may result in rejection of the bid as non-responsive.[284]

§ 8.6 WITHDRAWAL OF BIDS

Once its bid has been submitted, the bidder has made a binding offer for the contract work that the public entity can accept upon bid opening. A bidder may withdraw its bid by submitting a written request to the public entity before the deadline for bid submissions or, in some cases, before the bids are opened. A bidder who has withdrawn a bid may submit a new bid if the bid submission deadline has not already passed.[285]

§ 8.7 BID MISTAKES

A bidder who discovers that it has made a mistake in its bid after the bids have been opened can bring an action for any forfeited bid guarantee.[286] The action usually must be brought within ninety days of the bid opening.[287] The bidder must show that the mistake made a material difference in its bid. The bidder usually must notify the awarding public entity of the mistake within five days of the bid opening and must specify how the mistake occurred.[288] California courts have generally permitted successful bidders to rescind contracts based on bid mistakes involving clerical errors.[289]

§ 8.8 SUBLETTING AND SUBCONTRACTING FAIR PRACTICES ACT

The purpose of the Subletting and Subcontracting Fair Practices Act is to protect both the public and subcontractors from the practices of bid shopping and bid peddling in connection with public works projects.[290] Bid shopping and bid peddling usually result in poor quality service and lead to insolvencies and losses of wages, among other things.[291]

The Contract Code requires that bids include a list of the names and places of business of all subcontractors that will perform specified work on a public works project.[292]

If the prime contractor fails to specify subcontractors in its bid, it is assumed the prime contractor is fully qualified to perform and must perform the relevant portion of the work.[293] If a prime contractor fails to specify subcontractors, then fails to perform the relevant contract work, the prime contractor is subject to subcontractor substitution penalties and other penalties.[294]

Generally, a prime contractor may not substitute a subcontractor listed on its bid once the bid has been accepted.[295] However, the public entity may consent to substitutions under certain circumstances. Contract Code § 4107 permits subcontractor substitution in the following situations:

- When a listed subcontractor fails or refuses to execute a written contract.
- When a listed subcontractor becomes insolvent or bankrupt.
- When a listed subcontractor fails or refuses to perform a subcontract.
- When a listed subcontractor fails to meet the requisite bond requirements.
- When the prime contractor demonstrates to the awarding public entity that the name of the subcontractor was listed as the result of an inadvertent clerical error.
- When the listed subcontractor is not licensed.
- When the awarding public entity determines that the work performed by the listed subcontractor is substantially unsatisfactory.

Once a prime contractor has requested a substitution, but prior to approval by the public entity, the listed subcontractor is entitled to notice of the substitution and a hearing, if so requested in writing.[296]

The substituted subcontractor may have certain remedies against the prime contractor. For example, a substituted subcontractor may have a cause of action against the prime contractor for lost profits.[297]

R.J. Land & Associates Construction Company v. Kiewit-Shea, 81 Cal. Rptr.2d 615, (1999). In this case, a subcontractor (R.J. Land) was listed in a prime contractor's (Kiewit-Shea) successful bid, but was not actually used to doing the work it was supposed to do. The subcontractor sued the prime contractor under the Subletting and Subcontracting Fair Practices Act.

Although Kiewit-Shea did not intend to use R.J. Land for the work in question (they received a lower bid from another subcontractor at the last minute, and intended to use them instead of R.J. Land), it neglected to make the appropriate changes to its final bid submission.

The trial court granted Kiewit-Shea's motion for summary judgment, but the court of appeal reversed, stating that: (1)Kiewit-Shea had the opportunity to correct its final bid submission, and failed to do so, leaving R.J. Land as the listed subcontractor; (2)R.J. Land's ability to assert its rights under the Act was not barred simply because Kiewit-Shea made a mistake, as Kiewit-Shea argued at trial; and (3)issues in dispute should have precluded summary judgment.

§ 8.9 BID EVALUATION

New issues have arisen regarding public entities' discretion in evaluating bids. There is now a question whether public entities governed by low responsible bidder statutes have unrestricted freedom to award contracts based upon evaluations of various project alternatives as demonstrated below.

In a 1997 case[298], the trial court denied a contractor's petition for a writ of mandate challenging a city's use of alternative bidding for a construction project. The city divided the project into three phases and eventually determined that the cost of one phase would exceed its budget. The city separated the various elements of that phase, requested "base bids" for the portion of the phase the city was sure it wanted built, and also requested bids on nine alternatives so it could choose which of the alternatives would fit its budget. The plaintiff offered the lowest base bid, but after opening all the bids, the city decided that five alternatives were feasible and determined that in light of these chosen alternatives, another bidder was actually the lowest bidder. In entering a judgment for the city, the trial court found no evidence that the city had manipulated the award of the contract or violated applicable competitive bidding principles.[299]

The court of appeal reversed the decision and directed the trial court to inform the city that any alternative bidding procedure must ensure that the names of the bidders are kept confidential until after the city determines which alternative to include. The court held that the city's use of alternative bidding was not valid to the extent it allowed the city to choose alternatives after learning the bidders' identities.

Although the city's charter did not expressly authorize alternative bidding, the use of this procedure did not violate the city's competitive bidding law since it allowed the city to make the most economical use of its resources and deal with a problem in a sensible and practical way. However, the determination of alternatives after the bids were opened afforded the city an opportunity to favor a bidder and was, therefore not proper.[300] The court preliminarily held that the contractor's appeal was not rendered moot by the completion of the project since the city conceded that it used alternative bids at times and the issue of whether such a procedure violated competitive bidding laws was of continuing public interest.[301]

§ 8.10 PREVAILING WAGES

Bid invitations generally state that prevailing wages must be paid by general contractors and subcontractors on most public works projects in California. These wages are calculated and published by the Division of Labor Statistics and Research. If a contractor fails to pay these wages, it is liable to the public entity and the workers for repayment and fines, whether or not the contractor is a union contractor. It is common for all contractors on a particular project to sign a project labor agreement, whether they belong to a union or not. However, it is strongly recommended that specialized review of such an agreement be conducted to determine whether its provisions place nonunion contractors at a disadvantage in future labor-organizing activities or disputes.

A recent case[302] involved a painting subcontractor that was working under a public works contract between a county and a general contractor, and that violated the prevailing wage law. The labor commissioner issued an initial "notice to withhold," directing the county to withhold payment and penalties assessed at $50 per worker per day, the maximum statutory rate, from the general contractor based on the subcontractor's wage law violations. Although the commissioner ultimately concluded that the subcontractor's wage law violations were deliberate and fraudulent, and again assessed the maximum statutory penalty, the trial court granted the subcontractor's petition for a writ of mandate and set aside the initial notice to withhold as premature.[303]

The court of appeal reversed the trial court's decision, holding that the painting subcontractor possessed a "beneficial interest" and standing sufficient to maintain the mandamus proceeding, and that no adequate remedy at law was available (Code Civ. Proc., § 1086). The court of appeal also held that the trial court erred in setting aside the notice to withhold as premature. Although the commissioner did not determine the amount of penalties owed pursuant to Lab. Code § 1775 before issuance of the initial notice to withhold, the subcontractor forfeited underpaid wages and penalties when it violated the prevailing wage law. Hence, the county's power and duty to withhold penalties could be predicated on a preliminary or tentative estimation of penalties. Furthermore, the power to withhold funds is a device that can be used to aid in collection. The purpose of the 1989 amendments to Lab. Code § 1775 was not to impede the use of this device, but to increase the flexibility in its application.[304]

In another case,[305] the trial court granted a surety's motion for judgment on the pleadings in an action by the State of California Department of Industrial Relations, Division of Labor Standards Enforcement (DLSE), brought on behalf of workers on a public works project[306] for prevailing wages[307] against the surety that had furnished the payment bond required for the project. The trial court found that the action was barred by the ninety day statute of limitations of Lab. Code § 1775.[308]

The court of appeal reversed the decision, holding that the applicable limitations period was the six-month period of Civ. Code § 3249 (action against surety) and that the action was timely under that statute. The DLSE has the authority to bring an action on behalf of workers whose statutory rights to prevailing wages allegedly have been violated. Statutory provisions other that Lab. Code § 1775 also spell out the right to prevailing wages. Thus, the Lab. Code § 1775 remedy against the contractor is not the only means by which the DLSE may seek to collect prevailing wages under the prevailing wage law. Moreover, by its terms, Lab. Code § 1775 becomes applicable when the DLSE's suit is against a contractor, not another entity such as a surety. Thus, the ninety day limitation of Lab. Code § 1775 does not apply to an action for payment of prevailing wages against a surety on a payment bond.

In yet another case,[309] the trial court granted summary judgment for a contractor and related defendants in an action by the DLSE to recover unpaid wages for labor performed on a public works contract, based on the finding that the Employee Retirement Income Security Act (ERISA)[310] preempted California's prevailing wage law (Lab. Code § 1720 et seq.)[311]

The court of appeal reversed the judgment. The court held that in determining whether a state law relates to an ERISA plan because it has a "connection with" such a plan and is thus preempted, the court must consider whether the state law (1) regulates the types of benefits in ERISA employee welfare benefit plans; (2) requires that a separate employee benefit plan be established to comply with the law; (3) imposes reporting, disclosure, funding, or vesting requirements for ERISA plans; and (4) regulates certain ERISA relationships, such as those between an ERISA plan and an employer or between an employer and employee. Applying that test, the court held that the trial court erred in granting summary judgment for defendants.

The defendants were liable under the prevailing wage law, not because they failed to contribute to the employee benefit plan, but because they failed to pay their employees the prevailing wage. Where a legal requirement may be satisfied through means unconnected to ERISA plans, and relates only to ERISA plans at the election of an employer, it affects employee benefit plans in too tenuous, remote, or peripheral a manner to warrant a finding that the law "relates to" the plan, so as to be preempted. The prevailing wage law does not single out ERISA plans for special treatment, nor was it designed to affect such plans specifically. The provisions of the prevailing wage law at issue regulate wages generally and create no rights and restrictions predicated on the existence of any employee benefit plans.[312]

The prevailing wage law, which was designed to protect and benefit employees on public works projects, is an example of the broad authority states possess to protect workers.[313]

§ 8.11 BID PROTESTS - ADMINISTRATIVE CHALLENGES

Most bid protests are brought by unsuccessful bidders (typically the second lowest prime contractor or the second lowest subcontractor listed on the prime contractor's bid) after the public agency or staff has indicated its intent to award the contract. If a contractor does not immediately lodge a protest in writing to the public entity, the bid protest right may be waived.

Bid protest procedures vary with each public entity. Some procedures are informal and have not been put in writing.[314] However, the following steps are typical in bid protests handled by public entities:

§ 8.11.1 *Notice of Award*

The public agency opens the bids and notifies the public who will be awarded the contract.[315]

§ 8.11.2 *Request for Hearing and Notice*

Upon receipt of the notice of intention to award, any person or firm protesting the award must, within a certain period of time, file a written protest and request a hearing on that protest. The public agency then sets a time for the hearing.

§ 8.11.3 *Hearing and Decision*

Normally, witnesses are called and testimony is given. Generally, a transcript is made of the hearing. In addition, witnesses are often required to testify under oath even though the hearing is administrative. The public agency then makes a decision and gives notice of that decision.

§ 8.12 BID PROTESTS - LEGAL CHALLENGES

Several legal challenges are also available to an unsuccessful bidder when it has exhausted its administrative remedies and is not satisfied with a public agency's decision. The following are some examples of claims that may be alleged:

§ 8.12.1 *Interference with Prospective Economic Advantage*

Typically, a prime contractor awarded a contract may raise this claim against an unsuccessful bidder who is maliciously protesting the bid on the basis that the protest interferes with the prime contractor's economic interests.

§ 8.12.2 *Breach of Contract*

A *subcontractor* may allege an oral agreement with the prime contractor in which the prime contractor promised to use the subcontractor's bid in the proposal submitted to the public agency.

In addition, detrimental reliance by a bidder may be alleged on the theory of promissory estoppel.[316] Also, a subcontractor may have begun performance in accordance with a bid and would, therefore, have a claim for breach of contract with performance consisting of acceptance.

§ 8.12.3 *Abuse of Discretion*

Unsuccessful bidders often complain that public entities fail to properly follow applicable competitive bidding requirements. A disappointed bidder or any taxpayer may seek a writ of mandate to restrain a public body from awarding a contract to one other than the lowest responsible bidder if it can show the award is an abuse of discretion.[317]

Regarding this third legal challenge, a public entity has wide discretion in awarding public works contracts, as long as it exercises its discretion in good faith.[318] For example, the public entity may reject a low bid if it determines in good faith that the low bidder is not responsible.[319]

Under California law, a bid protester must demonstrate the awarding agency abused its discretion in awarding the contract. Abuse of discretion can be shown by demonstrating the public entity acted illogically, capriciously, or arbitrarily.[320] For example, a protestor may argue that the public entity failed to comply with competitive bidding requirements, *i.e.*, failed to award the contract to the lowest responsible bidder[321] or committed fraud based upon favoritism.[322]

Another abuse of discretion is collusion with other contractors. Most major projects require a certificate of non-collusion, whereby the bidder states under penalty of perjury that there was no collusion, including such things as bid rigging among the bidders or bribery of public officials to manipulate or control the bid.[323]

Finally, abuse of discretion may be shown by inappropriate quotas regarding minority, women, and disabled business enterprises. In the past, disabled business participation programs (DBEs) and minority business participation programs (MBEs) were upheld, and bidders that refused to comply with these quotas were rejected for non-responsibility. However, courts are increasingly refusing to enforce such programs unless the agencies can demonstrate a "firm basis for believing that remedial action is required."[324]

A public agency must narrowly tailor its MBE plan to specifically remedy past discriminatory practices. Otherwise, the plan fails under the equal protection clause of the U.S. Constitution.[325]

In <u>Associated General Contractors, Inc. v. San Francisco</u>,[326] the association challenged a city ordinance that permitted preferential hiring of minority, women, and local businesses, claiming that the ordinance violated the city charter, which required public works contracts to be awarded to the lowest bidder. The court cited <u>City of Inglewood</u>,[327] which interpreted the term "responsible" as being qualified to do the particular work under consideration with regard to quality, fitness, and capacity, only. The court refused to extend the scope of the term "responsible" to mean "socially responsible."[328]

Another recent case involving equal opportunity participation goals is <u>Domar Electric, Inc. v. City of Los Angeles</u>.[329] The court concluded the chartered city's requirement that bidders undertake good faith efforts to comply with minority participation goals in the bid process was not void because the goals were consistent with the competitive bidding goals and stimulated advantageous marketplace competition. Also, a bidder was not favored if the goals were met.

It is important to note that when a public works contract is governed by a statute calling for an award to the lowest responsible bidder, any hiring preferences will be closely scrutinized by the courts.

Chapter 9

CONSTRUCTION PITFALLS

The Old Quincy Courthouse
Courtesy University of California Library, Davis California

Summary:
Various aspects of contract performance are discussed, including scheduling, changes and modifications, suspension of work, project delays, payment and impossibility of performance. This chapter provides specific examples that may cause a suspension of work and discusses several types of delays, including excusable, inexcusable, compensable, and concurrent delays. With regard to payment, this chapter cites the applicable Contract Code Sections which discuss payment for performance and the ramifications of failure to pay. Three cases are cited in regard to excuses for Impossibility of Performance of contracts.

§ 9.1 Scheduling

Scheduling is an important aspect of any type of public works project. However, its role in claims and extensions of time in public works contracts is absolutely critical. The contract and resultant milestones and schedules provide expected completion dates and serve as the basis for coordination of the various subcontractors and trades involved. The series of approved and modified schedules, including as-bid, as-impacted, and as-built, are often utilized as the key documentation with regard to disputes over timely performance.

Two types of scheduling methods are used in the construction industry: the critical path method (CPM) and bar charts.

The **CPM method** depicts the flow of time and work. It identifies the critical activities of the project and the durations of each activity, along with critical deadline dates.

Bar charts are the more dated form of scheduling. The chart identifies the start and completion dates of particular activities, providing visual clarity. These charts are often prepared for presentation purposes, but are not as useful as the CPM.

Various construction phases and activities are identified and organized into these detailed schedules, which are updated as a project progresses. Typically, the contractor's equipment purchases, and completion or various phases of construction.

§ 9.2 Changes and Modifications

Construction contracts typically provide for changes by including a "change order" clause. Generally, the owner, architect, and contractor must agree on a change order. However, the owner has the right to direct a change in the work without an agreement with the contractor if the change is within the general scope of the contract. The architect alone has the authority to order any minor change in the work. The AIA General Conditions Form A201, Article 7, provides for such authority.

Construction contracts also typically include a requirement that all changes be in writing.[330] The parties can agree to waive the writing requirement; however, such a waiver will most certainly pose a major problem with regard to documentation if a dispute arises as to a particular change order request.

In addition to orders, "extras" play a large role in contractors' performance on public works construction projects. Extra work provisions may be inserted in contract by the public entity.[331] If the work to be performed is extraneous and not related to the original bid or contract, the contractor may have the right to refuse to perform, as beyond the scope of the contract.

If the contractor chooses to perform extra work, it will, of course, seek extra compensation. Public works contracts almost always provide for payment of extra work. Such provision typically requires a contractor to obtain a written extra work order that specifies the amount to be paid for the extra work and is signed by a public agency representative.[332] In addition, an extra work provision may be nullified if the contractor can show the public agency fraudulently concealed material facts.[333]

Numerous other provisions address the actual construction phase of a public works project. For example, the AIA General Conditions Form A201, Article 4.3.7, provides a standard provision for a claim for additional costs due to a change order. This provision states the contractor must submit a written estimate of the work prior to commencing with the change. Also, regarding extras, if the validity of an extra work claim is undisputed, Government Code § 980 provides for interest to be paid at a specified rate upon payment for the extra work.

§ 9.3 SUSPENSION OF WORK

A standard provision relating to suspension of work by an owner is set forth in the AIA General Conditions Form A201, Articles 14.3, 14.32. The provision states that the owner may suspend work in whole or in part for any duration of time. An adjustment will be made in the contract amount for any increases in costs caused by the suspension.

The following are a few examples of situations that may amount to a suspension of work:

- The failure of the city to proceed under a contract provision giving it the power to suspend work for an indefinite period amounted to a suspension of work.[334]

- The city's failure to provide required construction permits, easements, or rights-of-way required for construction to proceed in an orderly manner was determined to be a suspension of work.[335]
- The failure to act upon a contractor's request for information that was critical to the contractor's performance also amounted to a suspension of work.[336]

§ 9.4 DELAY

Delay may be the fault of the contractor or the public entity or due to other forces not within either party's control, such as weather. Both parties suffer damages as a result of any type of delay.

Typically, a contract will contain a provision specifying that the contractor is entitled to an extension of time if the delay is caused by forces outside its control.

Government Code § 53069.85 provides that cities, counties and districts can include a liquidated damages clause in their construction contracts for damages caused by a contractor's delay.[337] A standard provision regarding delays and extensions of time is contained in the AIA General Conditions Form A201, Article 8.3. California presumes the validity of reasonable liquidated damages clauses.

Several types of delays merit special discussion. Among those that most commonly occur are excusable, inexcusable, compensable, and concurrent delays.

An excusable delay is one that is unforeseeable, beyond the contractor's control, and not the fault of either party. Examples of excusable delays are Acts of God, strikes, unusually severe weather, and the inability of the contractor to obtain construction materials or fuel (as in the energy crisis in 1973 and 1974).

Excusable delays allow the contractor to obtain a time extension to complete the contract without being penalized. However, this type of a delay normally does not entitle the contractor to any damages caused by the delay.

If the delay is directly attributable to the contractor, the contractor is at fault and the delay is unexcused. Examples of an inexcusable contractor delay would be failure to order materials on time, inadequate staffing, and failure to coordinate subcontractors.

Typically, the liquidated damages clause in the contract will provide the public entity with a measure of assessing its damages caused by the contractors unexcused delay.

A compensable delay is one that is generally caused by the owner or its agents, such as the architect or engineer. Usually, the contractor will be entitled to an extension of time and has the right to recover damages due to the owner-caused delay. However, contracts vary in their approach to compensable delays, generally attempting to limit the recovery of the contractor except in extreme circumstances. As previously stated, public entities are limited in their ability to insert no damage for delay clauses in their contracts.

Examples of compensable delays are an owner's failure to make timely progress payments and issuance of numerous "stop work" and change orders,[338] and failure to make timely inspections of the property and to furnish materials on a timely basis.[339]

It may be difficult to determine which party is actually responsible for a delay because the delay of one party is intertwined with the delay by the other. In this case neither party may be entitled to recover damages from the other,[340] or, apportionment may be applied with the responsibility allocated between the parties.

§ 9.5 PAYMENT

A public works contract typically contains provisions regarding the payment of progress and final payments.[341] In addition, several statutory provisions apply to payments in the context of a public works project.

There was also the passage of Proposition 1A, known as SB50 or the "School Facilities Act of 1998." SB50 establishes the rules governing the financing and construction of new school facilities in California, including who pays what and when.

Public Contract Code §§ 10258 (payment where control is terminated or work abandoned), 10261 (payments upon contracts, progress payments), 102626 (payment to subcontractors), 10262.3 (Notice of progress payments to contractor), and 10264 (partial payment for mobilization costs) all relate to progress payments made to contractors and subcontractors by a state agency.

Public Contract Code § 10261, referred to as a "prompt pay statute," specifies that a state agency shall pay interest to a contractor at the rate of 10 percent per annum if the agency fails to make a progress payment within 30 days after receipt of the contractor's payment request.[342] Public Contract Code § 10262.5, also referred to as a "prompt pay statute," provides that any prime contractor that fails to make a progress payment to a subcontractor within 10 days from receipt of funds by the contractor must pay a penalty at the rate of 2 percent per month, in addition to interest.

Under Public Contract Code § 7107, retention payments withheld from payment by a public entity to an original contractor or by an original contractor to a subcontractor within 10 days after completion of the project (10 days after receipt of funds by the original contractor to a subcontractor). Failure to release such payments will result in a penalty assessed at the rate of 2 percent per month in lieu of interest.

§ 9.6 IMPOSSIBILITY OF PERFORMANCE

Impossible and impractical specifications are often encountered, especially in contracts governed by state contract law and in federal defense and energy contracts where the government is constantly pushing the state-of-the-art.

California law provides for an excuse of performance due to impracticality or impossibility of performance.[343] In fact, modern cases in California provide for an excuse from performance even when performance is impractical because of excessive and unreasonable difficulty or expense.[344]

In federal construction law, the excuse of performance principle has been established in cases such as Foster Wheeler v. United States,[345] where a required 19 - 24 month research and development period was clearly longer than the entire 13 month contractual performance period; Dynalectron Corp. v. United States,[346] where no contractor could manufacture certain antennas within the specified tolerances without significant waivers of the specification requirements; and Hol-Gar Manufacturing Corp. v. United States,[347] where no engine of the specified design could meet the performance requirements.

Chapter 10

ASSESSING DAMAGES

California State Building, Santa Rosa
Photo by Robert Brekke

Summary:

This chapter sets forth the legal criteria used to establish a breach of contract and the available damages or remedies. Determination of the time of the breach and application of the appropriate Statute of Limitations (CCP Section 337) is explained. Also included is the importance of documentation in order to establish the breach (See Chapter 13 Claims Analysis). The question of whether there is fraud or bad faith sufficient to establish a tort and claim exemplary damages is explored. Waiver of consequential damages - AIA approach and Eichleay Formula are discussed. Finally, the California False Claims Act (California Government Code Sections 12650-12655) and its applications are discussed.

§ 10.1 BREACH OF CONTRACT

Most construction claims arise out of a disagreement concerning the interpretation of a written agreement. Although most construction contracts in this day and age are relatively standard, the manner in which they are interpreted, and the differing site conditions to which they ostensibly must address, are diverse (and unpredictable). The authors of construction contracts are forever attempting to produce a contract which will meet the needs of the contracting parties while addressing, or at least setting forth, a procedure by which unforeseen events can be handled in a manner which will be expeditious and economical. However, when this fails, a claim ensues and the most prevalent theory under which claims are presented is breach of contract.

A breach of contract is generally defined as the unjustified, or unexcused, failure to perform a contract. Although ordinarily the breach of contract is the result of an intentional act, the negligent performance of a contract may also constitute a breach, giving rise to alternative contract and tort actions. We will address further in this chapter tort damages, but for the time being, let us direct our attention to purely contractual damages resulting from a breach.

The building industry generally involves contracts which provide for a payment by the owner to the contractor in installments based upon objective criteria specifically delineated within the contract itself; i.e., percentage of work completed. The question arises when one installment is not paid when it becomes due, whether or not this is a breach of contract. One view has been that the delay is only a temporary excuse for performance; i.e., the contractor may stop work until the progress payment is received, but he must resume work when paid, unless the delay is so unreasonably long as to amount to a material breach or failure of consideration, in which case it gives rise to the usual remedies of rescission or damages.

California courts have taken the approach that although a failure to pay an installment is not such a breach as to justify a suit for damages, the contractor may rescind (in effect, take back the contract) and recover the reasonable value of the work already done. There has been some discussion in the California courts regarding the somewhat inconsistent analysis of this rule, because if the delay is not serious, it should not justify termination of the contract. However, if it is serious and wrongful, it is a breach and damages are proper. The courts eventually found a reasonable approach, and have stated that there must be a "substantial" failure to comply with the terms of the contract for there to be a breach. Thus, an action for damages will lie for breach of contract if: (1) there was some act of prevention or hindrance by the owner; (2) or there is repudiation of the contract by the owner; or (3) the contract makes the timely payment of each installment an expressed condition precedent to the further duty of the performance of the remainder of the contract.

Thus, if the contract itself makes timely payment of each installment an expressed condition precedent to the further duty of performance by the contractor, then the contractor need not work if an installment is not made. However, the best rule of thumb is that barring an expressed condition in the contract, there must be a substantial deviation for a breach of contract to occur.

We can see from the outset that the most important area of assessing damages (or claims analysis) is to have a detailed review and understanding of the contract itself because these are the terms which will eventually "make or break" any claim. While researching the terms of the contract itself, it is essential that we keep in mind the time limitations upon which actions may be brought. (See Chapter 14, Deadlines and Time Deadlines.)

In this regard, Code of Civil Procedure §337 states the following:

> "Within four years: (1) An action upon any contract, or obligation or liability founded upon an instrument in writing, except as provided in Section 336(a) (an action upon any bonds, notes or debentures issued by a corporation) of this Code;"

Also, though not generally applicable, the "Oral Contract" Statute is:

> "Within two years: (1) an action upon a contract, obligation or liability not founded upon an instrument in writing..."

Thus, for general use, we must keep in mind that to bring a breach of contract action, it must be done within four years from the breach.

This, of course, begets the next question as to when does the breach occur.

In this regard, Civil Code §337 states that an action based upon rescission of a contract that is in writing must be filed within four years. The Code specifically states that the time begins to run from the date upon which the facts that entitled the aggrieved party to rescind occurred. Thus, there may be more than one breach of any given contract. As indicated under Chapter 13 entitled "Claims Analysis," it is important to document all of the acts and inactions which may or may not be tantamount to a breach so that the applicable date can be ascertained. For safety sake, one should always utilize the earliest possible date to protect oneself from the running of the statute of limitations.

The remedies for a breach of contract are numerous. Some of the remedies are: rescission and restitution; damages; specific performance; injunction; declaratory relief; ejectment for quiet title; as well as actions in tort which would result from a negligent breach or other wrongful conduct which may or may not be added as an alternative remedy to those found in contract.

Further, the contract itself may or may not specify the particular remedies that are available in the event of a breach, which may be in addition to, or in substitution of, those previously mentioned. However, keep in mind that a contract, or a provision in a contract, may attempt to limit the non-breaching parties' remedies. There are instances in which such a limitation has been upheld to limit the non-breaching party's damages to those specifically enunciated.

It has also been held by the courts in California that a party may waive a breach of contract and elect to treat the contract as still alive, remaining ready, willing and able to perform on his own part, and limiting his remedy to compensation for the breach. Also, a party may elect to treat a breach of contract as partial or total, and his damages would thus necessarily be effected.

Generally speaking, the damages to which one is entitled for a breach of contract are those damages which reasonably flow from the breach by the other party.

As indicated earlier, any claim, or breach of contract consists of two major parts. There is the entitlement section, which relies upon the specific provisions in the contract upon which the breach applies, as well as the damages section, which sets forth the calculations in support for the compensation claimed.

Some of the items of damage that have been awarded by the courts in construction claims dealing with a breach of contract are labor costs, equipment costs, material costs, bond and insurance costs, home office overhead, jobsite overhead, profit, interest and, if allowed within the contract documents itself, attorneys' fees.

As one can see, the basic object of damages is to compensate the party injured by allowing him, as nearly as possible, the equivalence of the benefits of performance. All damages must be proximately caused by the breach of the contract. This is a rule that has long been the law in England and the United States, and flows from the 1854 case of Hadley v. Baxendale, (9 Ex. 341, 156 Ang. Rptr. R. 145). That case dealt with general damages which naturally arise from the breach, or which might have been reasonably contemplated or foreseen by both parties, as well as special damages which arise from special circumstances and cause an unusual injury. Special damages are generally not recoverable unless the circumstances were known, or should have been known, by the guilty party at the time he entered into the contract.

Civil Code §3359 also provides:

> "Damages must, in all cases, be reasonable, and where an obligation of any kind appears to create a right to unconscionable and grossly oppressive damages, contrary to substantial justice, no more than reasonable damages can be recovered."

In early January 1998, Sears v. Baccaglio, 60 CA 4 1136, was decided by the First District Court of Appeals and dealt with who is a prevailing party in terms of collecting attorneys' fees on an action for breach of contract. The court found (pursuant to Civil Code §1717 and Code of Civil Procedure §1032) that the prevailing party in terms of who is entitled to attorneys' fees is that party who prevailed on **the contract**. The fact that one party might have "netted" more than another does not necessarily mean that the party who gets the most is the "prevailing" party.

§ 10.2 TORT DAMAGES

There are a number of situations in which, in a contractual obligation, there may be alternative tort action to which punitive damages may apply. These situations generally involve fraud or bad faith, and we find them most particularly in an insurance setting. As to whether or not tort damages would apply to any breach of contract, will rise and fall upon the facts surrounding the breach of contract itself. There are also specialized instances in which damages for physical injury or emotional distress may also apply to a breach of contract, such as associated with residential defects claims.

The Supreme Court will review a court of appeals which found that a homeowner can recover damages for emotional distress against a builder who constructed their home (Erlich v. Mensezes, 60 CA 4 1357, Second District Court of Appeals, 1998). (Review granted.)

The Supreme Court also granted review of Aas v. Superior Court, 98 C.D.O.S. 811, where the appellate court found that homeowners' as-sociations and individual homeowners do not have a private right of action in negligence against developers, general contractors and sub-contractors for recovery of economic losses they sustain as a proxi-mate result of construction defects in mass produced housing, including, but not limited to, those involving violations of governing building codes, which have not yet caused personal injury or physical damage to property, other than the defectively constructed portions of the residential structures themselves. The court further opined that the plaintiff may well have a negligence claim in the future, but only if the alleged latent construction defects result in physical harm to per-sons or other property within the 10 year limitation period. The court also disallowed residual loss of market value of the homes following repairs.

§ 10.3 WAIVER OF CONSEQUENTIAL DAMAGES

A waiver of consequential damages is contained in many construc-tion agreements. Others simply state a liquidated amount for project delay. As far as innovative approaches go, the AIA calls for the owner and the contractor to each waive what would otherwise be, in reality, consequential damages which would normally flow from the breach by either party. In the AIA approach, the contractor waives his home office overhead, which is often characterized as an indirect cost in the construction. It is not a direct cost, such as labor, materials and/or equipment, but typically includes the cost of accounting and payroll services, general insurance, the salaries of upper level management and marketing costs. The home office overhead is the actual dollar amount which is an essential part of the contractor's cost of doing business, thus he is giving up something in return for that which the owner waives. When dealing with the home office overhead, the standard, or formula, which is generally accepted in calculating this loss is the Eichleay Formula.

The owner, under the AIA approach, waives all potential economic loss associated with project delay. This would include extended construction interest and fees for extending the construction; increased interest on both the construction and permanent financing; extra licensing costs; lost revenues; and others.

In discussing damages, one must take into consideration that the non-breaching party is only entitled to that which he bargained for in the first instance. The non-breaching party is not entitled to be compensated in a manner which would put him in a better position had the breach not occurred. In this particular instance, this would be known as "betterment" and is not permitted.

§ 10.4 Fraudulent Claims

In 1987, the legislature enacted the California False Claims Act, which is codified in Government Code §§12650-12655. It provides a comprehensive statutory regulation of false and fraudulent claims "knowingly" submitted to state agencies or local public entities. It provides for civil penalties, as well as criminal penalties. The general understanding of these specific code sections is essential before presenting any claim to a public entity. The statute has the following definitions:

> "(2) `Knowing' and `knowingly' mean that a person, with respect to information, does any of the following:
>
> (a) Has actual knowledge of the information.
>
> (b) Acts in deliberate ignorance of the truth or falsity of the information.
>
> (c) Acts in reckless disregard of the truth or falsity of the information. Proof of specific intent to defraud is not required."

Thus, we see that specific intent to defraud is not necessary and the conscious disregard and utilization of false information can be actionable.

Chapter 11

PAYMENT REMEDIES

California State Court of Appeals, Riverside
Courtesy Swinerton & Walberg and A C Martin Partners, Inc.
Photo by LENOIR Photography

Summary:

The author explains in this chapter typical payment and collection remedies beginning with a written demand. He also discusses ceasing performance, filing a lawsuit, pre-judgment writ of attachment and self-help. In addition to these remedies, it is explained that the architect, engineer, general contractor, subcontractor and vendor have statutory rights as improvers of real property pursuant to the provisions of Civil Code Section 3084. Stop Notice requirements are discussed. A case cite is provided in a surety bond case brought on behalf of workers for nonpayment on a public works project.

§ 11.1 Who Has These Rights?

These rights are contained in the Civil Code, Sections 3084, et. seq. In general, any provider of labor, service, equipment, or material to a jobsite has the right to pursue a mechanic's lien, stop notice, and payment bond right. However, the rules for these procedures are very strict, and careful compliance with the statutes, and legal advice, is required to perfect these rights.

§ 11.2 Preliminary Notice

As a general matter, a claimant under these statutes (other than an original contractor or persons performing actual labor for wages), must file a Preliminary Notice in order to have any mechanic's lien rights. This must be filed within 20 days of providing labor, services, or equipment. Civil Code 3097 (a). The notice must be served upon all interested parties, although failure to serve one party may only defeat the right against that party. In general, the owner, lender, and all upper tier contractors should be served with the Preliminary Notice. These forms are generally available, but they must be checked against current statutory requirements.

In re Baldwin Builders, 99 C.D.O.S. 2248, (1999). The bankruptcy court held that a creditor's post-petition suits to enforce a mechanics' lien were in violation of the automatic stay. The Bankruptcy Appellate Panel affirmed.

Here, Southern Counties Landscape (SCL) gave notice of a mechanics' lien against baldwin Builders before Baldwin actually filed for bankruptcy. After Baldwin filed, SCL sued to foreclose two different times, but failed to give notice to Baldwin or its trustee in both occasions.

As the only purpose for SCL's foreclosure attempts was "to maintain or continue perfection", an action that § 546 (b) of the Bankruptcy Code says requires notice, the foreclosure suits were found to be void.

§ 11.3 The Mechanic's Lien

The mechanics' lien is a security interest against private real property. It is almost never available against public property. It must be the property that is being improved. by the claimant. The mechanic's lien must contain a demand after payments and offsets, a description of the real property, the name of the reputed owner, the person who employed the claimant, and a verification. Civil Code Section 3084.

The lien must be filed by the general contractor within 60 days of a valid note of completion or notice of cessation is recorded. The general has 90 days from completion if no notices are filed regarding completion or cessation. Subcontractors have 30 days after recording of a notice of completion or cessation. A Notice of Completion must be filed within 10 days of actual completion to be valid. The date of recording starts the time period.

Mechanic's liens are only available against private property. There are no mechanic's liens against public improvements. However, private lease interests in public property may be liened.

Schmitt v. Tri Counties Bank, 99 C.D.O.S. 2228, (1999). The court of appeal affirmed a trial court decision, holding that a contractor's (Northstate Asphalt) site improvement lien had priority over a lender's (Tri Counties Bank) recorded deed of trust.

While recorded deeds generally have priority over mechanics' liens, Civil Code Section 3137 gives priority to site improvement liens unless the lender ensures that all site improvement liens are satisfied before releasing any funds.

Here, Country National Bank, and its successor, Tri Counties Bank, both failed to comply with the relevant portions of section 3137. Consequently, Tri Counties Bank's deed of trust was not afforded priority over the site improvement lien of Northstate.

§ 11.4 ENFORCEMENT OF MECHANIC'S LIENS

A lawsuit to enforce the mechanic's lien must be commenced no later than 90 days from the date of recording the lien. There is a statutory mechanism, called a "Notice of Credit," for extending this period for another 90 day period. If the lawsuit is not timely filed, the mechanic's lien is void. There is a statutory procedure for removing an invalid lien, involving notice to the claimant, and award of attorneys' fees if the claimant does not execute a release of lien.

The waiver of a mechanic's lien right must exactly follow the statutory release form or risk being held invalid. The release forms, drafted by the legislature, leave much to be desired. As such, many contractors and owners require a series of side letters and other documentation in addition to the lien release.

§ 11.5 PUBLIC PROJECT MECHANIC'S LIENS (RARE)

Mechanic's lien rights do not apply to public works projects.[348] However, if title to any of the real property involved in a public project is held by private owners rather than a public agency, general contractors, subcontractors, or material suppliers may place a lien on the project. This issue can also arise in redevelopment projects or private ground lease situations. In fact, a mechanic's lien can be filed against virtually any privately held real property interest, including boat slip contracts and air rights agreements. However, the public agency has immunity against mechanic's liens filed on any public-owned real property itself.

§ 11.6 BONDS AND STOP NOTICE REQUIREMENTS

A very important area of evaluating claims and assessing liability is the issue of bonds and stop notice requirements for public entities.

Claimants may be secured in contracting with public agencies by means of payment bonds or stop notices. A stop notice is a form of garnishment and is accomplished by a written notice, signed and verified by the claimant or its agent. The notice must state the type of work performed and of the work agreed to be performed.

Civil Code § 3098 provides requirements for subcontractors or material suppliers to file a preliminary 20-day notice with a public entity in order to preserve stop notice rights on a public works project. Once the preliminary notice has been filed, the subcontractor or material supplier may file the stop notice. Upon receipt of a stop notice, the public agency or construction lender is obligated to withhold money due the contractor to satisfy the claim. The time for filling a stop notice is set forth in Civil Code § 3184. By filing a stop notice with the owner or construction lender, a subcontractor or supplier gains a lien against the construction funds that would otherwise be paid to the claimant's alleged debtor. In order to recover on a stop notice, a suit must be filed. The time requirements for filing such a suit are set forth in Civil Code §§ 3210-3212.

When the validity of a stop notice is in dispute between a contractor and a subcontractor, a stop notice may be released by the public entity by allowing the prime contractor to file a bond. The public entity then releases the stop notice and disburses the money withheld pursuant to such notice.[349] The subcontractor's cause of action is then on the bond, not on the stop notice.[350]

In addition, the prime contractor awarded a public works contract is required to post a payment bond with the public entity if the contract is in excess of $25,000.[351] The amount of the payment bond to be posted varies, depending upon the contract amount.[352] In order to recover on the payment bond, a claimant must provide a 20-day written notice.[353] Other requirements for filing an action on the payment bond are also set forth in the same statutes. A suit must be filed in a timely manner to perfect a claim on the payment bond.

Chapter 12

THIRD PARTY CLAIMS

San Francisco Hall of Justice
Photo by Robert Brekke

Summary:
Death or injury to construction workers on the job and Worker's Compensation remedies are discussed. In addition, third-party claims, indemnity and insurance issues for the general contractor or owner are explained. Equipment and product failure as a form of strict liability are also discussed, in addition to claims for construction defects. A list of typically claimed defects is provided. Also included in this chapter are the issues of liability for grading and subsurface defects and allegations of nuisance and trespass, as well as insurance coverage and reservation of rights.

Generally, third-party claims involve personal injury or property damage to members of the general public.

Some are of the nuisance variety. One example is the classic "paint over spray" cases that involve hundreds of cars parked adjacent to the jobsite. One case reportedly resulted in more claims than spaces in the parking lot. Even without fraud, dust, paint and rock cases can be expensive on prolonged jobs

But third-party claims can be economically lethal to owners, general contractors, subcontractors and design firms.

§ 12.1 Construction Accident Claims

Injury or death of construction workers is a serious problem in the industry. Due to the youth and relative high pay of these workers, injury and death claims can be financially devastating. The severity of this problem in California has been uniquely threatening, as described below.

§ 12.1.1 Workers' Compensation

Under The California Labor Code, the injured worker is entitled to worker's compensation benefits associated with any workplace injury, so long as it was incurred during the course of employment.

In addition, this remedy, which is required by law to be afforded by employers, is intended to be the exclusive remedy against the employer, except in extreme circumstances (physical attack by a supervisor, etc.).

§ 12.1.2 Third-Party Lawsuits

However, due to the multi-employer nature of the construction industry, there are almost always other employers, such as the general contractor, subcontractors, vendors, and, of course, the owner, that the injured employee is free to sue. Generally, the employee will argue that those other companies, and their employees, caused or contributed to his or her injury. Claims of negligence or strict liability against these entities results in numerous parties being brought into the lawsuit.

§ 12.1.3 *Indemnity and Insurance Issues*

Once the owner, general contractor or other defendant is brought into the suit, they will tend to tender defense and indemnity of the suit to the employer of the injured worker. Generally, that will be a lower tier subcontractor, since most workers are so employed. Those lower tier employers generally have indemnified the owner and general contractor, as well as the architect and others, against just this type of suit. In addition, their insurance companies often are required to add the owner, general contractor, and others to their insurance polices as additional insureds.

As a result, the lower tier subcontractor is often denied the benefit of the worker's compensation exclusive remedy statute. When the liability insurance and umbrella of the subcontractor is exhausted, the other parties must respond in damages and the subcontractor may be forced to find refuge in the bankruptcy courts. It is risky situation for these subcontractors, and yet another reason to assure jobsite safety at all costs.

§ 12.1.4 *Products Liability Issues*

Other jobsite accidents may involve construction equipment or manufactured products. These cases are very affected by the fact that products liability is considered a form of strict liability. There need not be fault. Under current law, a product may be defective in manufacture or in design. There are two tests for design defects: one is a design that is simply defective in that it does not work, and two, that once some aspect of the design is found contributory to the accident, then the burden of proof shifts to the manufacturer to prove that the design was reasonable. In addition, failure to warn can be found a design defect. Thus, the lack of a simple warning can result in strict liability.

§ 12.2 CONSTRUCTION DEFECT CLAIMS

§ 12.2.1 *Prevalence in Residential Construction*

As mentioned previously, construction defect litigation is a growth industry in California. The legal theory used against each defendant will depend on the nature of the defendant's involvement in the project.

The architect, engineer and contractor will most often be sued for professional negligence and ordinary negligence, respectively. In addition, the general contractor and subcontractors will be sued for breach of warranty, express and implied, and for breach of contract, as well as the occasional fraud or misrepresentation allegation.

§ 12.2.2 *Typical Defect Claims*

One industry source cites the following as typical types of defect claims on residential and commercial improvements:

> The action of consolidating or expansive soils
>
> Inadequate soils testing
>
> Failure to meet code requirements
>
> Inadequate ADA Compliance
>
> Extreme topographic conditions
>
> Inadequate site preparation
>
> Improper foundation design for soils or topography
>
> Unsatisfactory placement of backfill
>
> Poor finish grade and drainage
>
> Poor landscaping techniques
>
> Improper tree and plant selection
>
> Incorrectly designed and installed water protection
>
> Poor moisture barriers and flashing
>
> Framing errors, especially seismic bracing
>
> Improper nailing patterns
>
> Inappropriate or inferior materials
>
> Failure to follow manufacturer installation requirements
>
> Poor workmanship - inexperienced tradesmen
>
> Insufficient monitoring by superintendent
>
> Lack of adequate testing or quality assurance
>
> Lack of risk management effort
>
> Failure to properly document condition of property
>
> Poor punch list and repair responsiveness

§ 12.2.3 *Strict Liability for Mass Graded Lots & Tract Housing*

The developer of mass graded lots can also sued for strict liability. Kreegler v. Eichler, 269 Cal Rptr 224 (1969). In addition, that liability extends to strict liability for defective subsurface conditions resulting from improper filling and grading. Avner v. Longridge Estates, 272 Cal App 2d 607 (1969). Where the problem is continuing, allegations of nuisance and trespass are regularly pursued.

§ 12.2.4 *Insurance Coverage Issues*

As discussed in Chapter 6, construction defect claims raise very technical and difficult coverage issues. The existence or lack of insurance coverage, or even a defense, is often referred to as the life's blood of the litigation process.

The classic insurance policy language regarding coverage is along these lines: "We (the insurance company) will pay those sums that the insured becomes legally obligated to pay as damages because of ... 'property damage' ... which occurs because of ... 'property damage' ... which occurs during the policy period ... caused by an occurrence."

Insurance carriers often attempt to deny construction defect claims stating there was not personal injury or property damage, that there was no "occurrence," or that there is no coverage for purely economic losses.

In addition, the carriers generally allege that the policies do not cover purely contractual or warranty issues, or the product or workmanship of the insured.

Each policy and each claim is unique. A thorough policy analysis can often persuade an insurance carrier that, in fact, the loss is covered. Also, the duty to defend is broader than the duty to pay the claim.

Beware the insurance company that provides a defense, under a reservation of rights, then asks for reimbursement after the fact for defense costs. Always press the insurance company for a commitment not to seek reimbursement, even if you must agree that the issue of coverage of the ultimate claim is not yet resolved. Otherwise, the insured and insurance company will be adverse, and highly distrustful of each other, through the entire proceeding.

Construction insurance coverage for defects is a highly technical area. These are just a few of the issues that are regularly litigated in the so called "case within a case" of insurance coverage litigation.

Chapter 13

CLAIMS ANALYSIS

Los Angeles County Courthouse
Courtesy Los Angeles Superior Court

Summary:
This chapter introduces basic claims analysis, including preparing a chronology, hiring of technical expert witnesses, and review of all relevant financial records. The importance of conducting a thorough investigation of the facts, including preparation of a roster of all claim participants, are discussed. Instructions for a thorough review of the contract, plans, specifications and applicable issues of indemnity and insurance, the benefit of obtaining taped statements from witnesses, and video taping construction sites (including narration) are provided. Finally, this chapter discusses that knowing representation of a false claim may cause disbarment of the contractor from future public business and may also result in civil penalties for each false claim.

§ 13.1 Suggested Claims Approach: Phasing the Analysis

The evaluation of construction claims by counsel may be divided into the following three phases of work:

- Phase I, confirming that the contractor's claims have been submitted in accordance with specifications of the prime contracts and summarizing essential allegations.

- Phase II, preparing in-depth reports, chronologies, calculations, recommendations, strategy, summaries, and updates when requested by the client.

- Phase III, where prior resolution is not achieved, providing the client with assistance in the mediation, arbitration, or litigation of the contractor's claims.

§ 13.1.1 *Phase I: The Factual Investigation*

The factual investigation of a public works claim is crucial. A well-organized, thoughtful investigation will provide the client the information that will increase the likelihood of a cost-effective resolution of any claims on the project.

The most important aspect of this investigation, as well as subsequent claims analysis, is to have a systematic plan so that the hundreds (or thousands) of hours spent can be applied to the most productive and useful tasks possible. The quality of the factual investigation will greatly assist in negotiating or litigating claims from a position of knowledge and strength.

The specific tasks to be performed in the factual investigation are many and include contract review, statutory notice, plans and specifications review, review of indemnity and insurance issues, and meetings with the various players involved with the project. The following is a brief description of the tasks involved:

§ 13.1.1(a) *Project Roster*

Immediately upon retention should create a project roster containing key information about the project and distribute it to all of the professionals. This roster should serve as the project encyclopedia for all claim participants. It will save time later in the claim process as basic project information is needed and will assist each participant in quickly learning the particularities of the project. The roster should be updated from time to time as the analysis progresses.

The project roster should include the prime contract, as well as the names, addresses, telephone numbers, and project roles of the designers, consultants, contractors, subcontractors, inspectors, testing agencies, and material suppliers. It should also list all state and federal funding agencies (which may trigger state and federal agency regulations regarding claim submission, award of contracts, and audit requirements for approved claims), any cooperating government entities, notices of acceptance/completion and the resulting dates by which stop notices must be filed, and the names of sureties and insurance policies issued in favor of the client.

§ 13.1.1(b) Project Issues List

The key organizational tool is a project issues list. The subjects on this list are usually gleaned from contractor's and agencies' written claims, depending on the format required by the contract and specifications.

A claim issue file should be created from the project issues list. The claim issue file typically includes issue background, issue chronology, the contractor's position and supporting documentation of damages, and the public agency's position and supporting documentation regarding merit and damages. This file should also include an analysis of the likelihood of each party prevailing on the issue, the probable range of results of an award, and the estimated costs of arbitrating or litigating such an issue. The suggested method of resolution should also be included in the index (e.g., fixed offer, negotiation range, mediation, arbitration, or litigation).

With regard to each identified project issue, a supporting physical file should be established for all written material and evidence gathered in support of that issue. In addition, the project issue file is the cornerstone for building a computer index, if needed, of all project documents and interviews.

The project issues list and files should include all major technical, quality of work, delay and economic claims of the contractors and subcontractors involved in the work in question.

§ 13.1.1(c) Contract Review

All relevant contracts must be read in full. The prime contract and general conditions for each specific project will constitute the " road map" for the judge or arbitrator. The signing of these contracts may have been the last time the parties agreed, so their contents are vital.

§ 13/1/1(d) Contractual Requirements

Since many agencies are concerned about increases in project costs, their contracts typically place a great deal of responsibility on the general contractor to provide early warning and cost documentation regarding potential delays and claims of the project. Such notice clauses are important for the well-being of both the contractor and the public agency and can lead to sever prejudice to the contractor's claim if they are not followed.

The contractor's claim may, in certain circumstances, be considered null and void if it fails to comply with the notice requirements contained in the contract and the applicable statutes. These provisions generally contain strict time limits for the contractor to give such notice.

Conversely, an otherwise valid counterclaim may be lost due to non-compliance with the offset or final payment provisions of the project construction agreement. Failure to adhere to such requirements may prove fatal to the construction claims of the parties. This is covered in more detail in Chapter 14.

§ 13.1.1(e) Plans and Specifications Review

The public agency's plans and specifications must be reviewed by an independent consultant. The project management team and project engineers should then be interviewed in depth on key issues. An early site visit is recommended, preferably with the project manager, project engineer, and the engineer or architect who designed the project. Videotaping of the site inspection, with narration by the project manager, is advisable. A videotape is especially useful if the project is still under construction or if particularly troublesome punch list items need to be shown. Several rolls of slide film should also be used to document site conditions.

§ 13.1.1(f) Indemnity and Insurance

There should be an early review of the insurance policies and indemnity agreements — both can shift construction losses. Coverage can be found in unusual places. For example, the public agency may have been named as an additional insured on the general contractor's or subcontractor's policy. Being named as an additional insured may entitle the public agency to defense costs and insurance coverage if early notice is given to the insurance carrier. If the involved carrier is notified too late, it may be able to claim prejudice, which would result in the loss of an otherwise valid coverage claim in favor of the public agency.

§ 13.1.1(g) Key Witness Interviews

Interviewing the public agency's personnel and other project key witnesses in person and on audio cassette tape, with their permission, is a powerful information-gathering tool. The tapes can be transcribed and entered into the litigation support system. Key witnesses often include project inspectors, outside design consultants, staff members from the public agency most directly involved in the project, and any knowledgeable third-party witnesses willing to speak candidly. Such interviews have proven to be invaluable: the witnesses provide colorful description and analogies that can be used to strengthen one's position.

The resulting transcripts serve as a project resource and reference for the claim. The key sections of the transcripts can be used in correspondence and declarations in support of motions and trial briefs.

§ 13.1.1(h) Contractor — Public Agency Meeting

Following the initial Phase 1 assessment, it is useful for counsel to arrange a meeting between the contractor and public agency staff to listen carefully and firsthand to opposing views of the claim. Information not present in the claim can also be requested or obtained during such a meeting.

§ 13.1.2 *Phase II: Detailed Claims Analysis*

The breadth of analysis set up in Phase I is actually carried out in Phase II. To ensure that expenditures for the claims analysis are optimized, it is suggested that Phase II be organized in two parts. The first part of Phase II ends at a distinct milestone at which a broad, but limited, analysis of the claim has been completed and a settlement of the claim or individual issues may be negotiated, thus eliminating the need for further analysis. On the other hand, if a settlement cannot be achieved at this juncture, nothing has been lost, and the analysis continues in greater depth.

The following is a brief description of the tasks included in Phase II:

§ 13.1.2(a) Project Chronology

The chronological sequence of events serves initially as an organizational tool. Later, excerpts from project documents and interviews can be added to the chronology.

§ 13.1.2(b) Financial Records Review

The financial records of the project and all contractors should be reviewed. This information can be obtained by agreement, pursuant to an audit clause, or through court-ordered discovery. The team will also meet with the project financial officer and the contracts administration group.

California case law is fairly strict about the degree of certainty needed to prove construction damages. The public agency staff may not know the full financial impact of a delay on public agency operations and reviews, so this analysis should be undertaken well in advance of serious settlement discussions. An early indication of the settlement value of the claim will provide the budget blueprint as to the analysis, organization, and negotiation of the claim. Counsel will need to know quickly whether the records gathered will meet the burden of proof or whether expert witnesses will be needed to testify as to damage issues.

§ 13.1.2(c) Technical Analysis and Early Expert Witness Involvement

Construction industry disputes are generally extremely technical in nature. As a result, experts should be brought in early to shape the strategy and avoid surprises. They must be able to stand up under cross examination with credibility, and, if possible, in an effort to mitigate costs, each expert should be able to address several areas of the claims.

§ 13.1.2(d) Calculation of Quantum

For each finding of entitlement, a calculation of quantum (the portion to which each party is entitled) is made. The approach may be to make a completely independent determination or simply to check the claimants' calculations and review supporting documentation.

§ 13.1.3 Phase III: Other Available Avenues to Pursue

If a claim is not resolved after Phases I and II have been completed, mediation, negotiation, or other means of settlement may be utilized, as summarized below.

§ 13.1.3(a) Advantages to Early Settlement

The most important advantage to early settlement is money. Few public agencies or contracting firms can afford a lengthy trial or arbitration. Large construction cases are expensive to bring to trial. The administrative expense of being involved in such cases often exceeds the attorneys' fees and experts' costs. These costs are burdensome to public agency operations and can put a medium-size construction or design firm out of business.

§ 13.1.3(b) Planning the Mediation/Negotiation

General contractors often do a poor job of communicating the factual basis of their claims to public agency staff and outside consultants involved in analyzing the claims. Many adopt an aggressive negotiation approach that may work with the subcontractors, but are unable to come to the negotiation table ready to discuss "give and take."

A contractor's lack of effectiveness in attempting to resolve a claim early should not prevent the public agency from taking the initiative to determine the fair value of the claim, the amount owed to the contractor, and the costs to be subtracted from the amount owed. The contractor will most likely wish to reach an early settlement to ensure the company's cash flow.

The administrative and budgetary constraints in an action by a public agency may be difficult for a contractor to understand. It is the goal of the agency to conserve and protect public funds, achieve the stated project quality objectives, and meet the project time schedule. It is the public agency's mandate to establish a clear written record to support all change orders and requests for extension. Because of these factors, an early well-documented approach by the public agency in evaluating the contractor's claims for cost increases and extensions of time is suggested. Successful claim negotiation can occur only in a business environment where facts are discussed.

The foregoing approach is presented for illustrative purposes only, and may not be appropriate for every claim situation.

§ 13.1.3(c) Selecting the Negotiation Team

The most important decision in pursuing early resolution of a claim is the selection of a negotiation team. Both sides must come to the table with bargaining authority and a willingness to reach a compromise. The ideal team should include a senior individual involved in the project, counsel familiar with the major claims, and a seasoned claim consultant.

§ 13.1.3(d) Settlement Agenda

The parties should agree upon a settlement process agenda and schedule sequential meetings on specific claim items. Negotiations for large claims require the careful planning, so discussions must proceed systematically. Back up documentation and information should be available to fully complement the negotiation process.

One approach to the settlement agenda is to proceed from the most objective issues to the most subjective. For instance, an effective sequence might be to begin at the beginning: changes in the plans and specifications. From there, changes to the scope of work should be discussed, followed by the remaining punch list items. Delays and disruptions affecting the completion schedule should be next on the agenda. The last issues for discussion should be the resultant impact of all items on the schedule and the delay claims. Even if the final issues on the agenda preclude complete settlement, this approach significantly narrows the scope of the dispute.

§ 13.1.3(e) The Settlement

When a negotiated settlement has been reached, counsel will generally prepare a comprehensive settlement agreement resolving all related issues. A settlement agreement will include the method of payment, future warranty, indemnity, stop notices, and confidentiality. A lengthy settlement meeting should not end until the resolved issues are put in writing and given to all participants.

The parties should always keep in mind that a failure to settle a construction dispute as soon as possible can result in protracted litigation. Aggregate costs to all parties can approach a large amount when a matter becomes embroiled in litigation. The goal should be to reach a fair and equitable settlement, with litigation being the last resort.

§ 13.2 FALSE CLAIMS

A final aspect of claims analysis that is critical for both the public entity and construction industry professionals is the California False Claims Act of 1987 (FCA), set forth in Government Code §§ 12650 - 12655. This act, which is similar to the Federal False Claims Act (18 U.S.C.A. § 287), provides for the regulation of false and fraudulent claims submitted to state and local public agencies.

In the past, a contractor that knowingly submitted a false or fraudulent claim to a public entity was only subject to criminal fines and penalties.[354] The FCA establishes civil penalties and fines for the same conduct, thus making another remedy available to public entities.

If a contractor knowingly submits a false claim to a public entity, it will be liable for three times the amount of damages that the entity sustains, the costs of the suit and a civil penalty of up to $10,000 for each false claim.[355]

Filing a false claim can also result in temporary or permanent debarment of a contractor from future business with one or more public entities. Debarment is often called "the death penalty for contractors." A recent example of the process is set forth in <u>Stacy & Witebeck, Inc. v. City of San Francisco</u> (1995) 36 Cal. App. 4th 1074, 44 Cal. Rptr. 2d 472. Pursuant to a section of a city administrative code, the city's public utilities commission (PUC) deemed a contractor to be an irresponsible bidder due to its filing of a false claim under a construction contract and banned it from bidding on city public works projects for five years. The contractor petitioned for injunctive relief. The trial court, which determined that the distortions in the claim did not violate any of the provisions governed by the city's administrative code section and, hence, that the PUC lacked any legal basis for issuing its order, granted a preliminary injunction enjoining the city and the PUC from enforcing the order. (Superior Court of the City and County of San Francisco, No. 961-598, William J. Cahill, Judge.)

The court of appeal reversed the order granting the preliminary injunction. The court held that the action of the PUC in deeming the contractor to be an irresponsible bidder was valid under the City's administrative code. The city charter charged the PUC with the construction, management, operation, and control of all public utilities. The PUC carried out this charge pursuant to a chapter of the code entitled "Contract Procedure," which permitted the PUC to deem a contractor irresponsible for failing to abide by rules and regulations set forth in the chapter. Further, the PUC properly ruled that the covenant for good faith and fair dealing was an implicit requirement of the clause of the contract under which the contractor's claim was made and, thus, of the code section governing payment of such claims. Moreover, the court held that the city's appeal of the trial court's injunction was not void even though the code section under which the order was made had been repealed, and that the code section was not facially unconstitutional, even though it did not specifically delineate any procedures for notice and hearing followed by the PUC at the hearing were fair.

The court also held that the claim for contract overages submitted to the city by the contractor could serve as the basis for the administrative action by the PUC to declare the contractor an irresponsible bidder, despite the contractor's contention that the claim was absolutely privileged under Civil Code § 47, subd. (B) (litigation privilege) because it had been filed in connection with underlying litigation between the contractor and the city. Finally, the court held that state law did not preempt either (1) the code section that provided for declaring a public works contractor an irresponsible bidder or (2) the action of the PUC thereunder in declaring the particular contractor an irresponsible bidder. (Opinion by Anderson, P. J., with Poche and Perley, JJ., concurring.)

A second decision the following year, <u>Stacy & Witebeck, Inc. v. City and County of San Francisco</u> 47 Cal. App. 4th 1, 54 Cal. Rptr. 2d 530 [No. A067893. First Dist., Div. Four. Jul 2,1996.], addressed the trial courts granting summary adjudication in favor of the contractor on the FCA cause of action, ruling that the alleged false claim was absolutely privileged under Civil Code § 47, subd. (b), since it was submitted to the city in anticipation of litigation. The trial court had entered judgment accordingly.

The court of appeal, thereafter, reversed the trial court's judgment. The court held that the city's cross complaint was not barred by the Civil Code § 47, subd. (b), litigation privilege. Although the contract claim followed the contractor's presentation to the city of its claim under the Tort Claims Act (TCA) for material breaches of contract and subsequent rejection of the TCA claim, the contractor initiated its breach of contract action for the alleged damages detailed in the contract claim. The filing of the contract claim was also called for under the contract, and it stood wholly apart from any judicial action. Further, even though Government Code § 12652, subd. (e), excludes from liability claims made under TCA, the contractor had also filed a separate contract claim. Thus, while the TCA claim was an independent item with statutory requirements governing its contents (Government Code § 910), the contract claim did not resemble the claim described in Government Code § 910, and was required pursuant to both the terms of the contract and the course of dealing between the parties. While the contract claim ultimately served a litigation purpose as well, it clearly was not a claim, record, or statement made pursuant to the TCA.

Chapter 14

DEADLINES AND LIMITATIONS

Old Mendocino County Courthouse, Ukiah
Courtesy University of California Library, Davis California

Summary:

Legal notice requirements in private and public contracts are discussed in this chapter. Strict adherence to claim notice requirements is required to forestall a waiver of the claim rights. Notice of delay is discussed and that the courts strictly construe any delay of the required notice, especially if such delay prejudices the other party so that its impact can be ascertained. Statutory notice requirements are discussed pursuant to California Government Code Section 1000 <u>et.</u> <u>seq</u>. Contract claims in public works projects (California Government Code Section 9201) and Alternative Dispute Resolution are explored, in addition to miscellaneous statutes of limitations that may apply.

§ 14.1 CONTRACT PROVISIONS

The following is a summary of the **legal notice requirement**s governing claims most often encountered in private and public contracts.

A **notice of claim** must be provided to the public entity by the entity who is filing the claim. While many contractors feel notice clauses are just an attempt to place one more hurdle in the path of valid claims, the intent of such clauses is to provide the public agency an opportunity to address the potential claim by eliminating the cause of the claim, deleting troublesome scope of work items, or reducing the impact of delays. Notice clauses also allow the agency to begin to build a record in order to defend itself from the claim.

In those instances where the contractor has not given the required notice of potential delay and claims, the courts have often denied the contractor relief to which it would otherwise be entitled. Therefore, the contractor must strictly adhere to the claim notice requirements to prevent a waiver of its claim rights. A careful reading of all notice provisions at the outset of the claims review process will reveal all applicable notice provisions.

Most construction contracts contain provisions requiring a contractor to give prompt notice of a claim to enable public agency staff to take appropriate protective measures. This notice is typically termed "notice of delay."

Certain courts have strictly construed such **notice of delay** clauses, barring claims for time extensions or delay damages to contractors who fail to give timely notice. However, in the view of more liberal courts, failure to comply with notice clauses should not cause a forfeiture of the claim if the public agency is not prejudiced. The determination of prejudice may turn on whether the public agency did, in fact, have notice of the claim, so it could minimize the impact on the contractor and begin to collect data on the claimed increase in costs.

Many contracts require the contractor to provide immediate notice when any **unanticipated or concealed condition** is encountered during the course of the work. These clauses allow the public agency to inspect concealed conditions and, in certain cases, issue design modifications or change orders that may tend to minimize project disruption.

Disputed work is often the heart of a claim. Standard specifications generally require daily reports to the engineer on all labor, materials and equipment involved for any extra work claimed by the contractor.

Requests for an appeal are another important issue. Project agreements tend to empower the engineer, architect, or other agent of the public agency to initially determine the validity of a contractor's claim. If the contractor wishes to contest such an entity's decision, certain clauses may require an immediate **request for appeal** to be filed by the contractor.

A notice of termination for default (or convenience) may be required, as well, by the terms of the contract documents. In extremely difficult situations, where the contractor is in material default on the contract or where the public agency is unable to perform, the affected party may be forced to give **notice of termination for default**. Events that may call for a notice of termination include an agency's inability to provide job site access, an agency's failure to make the agreed progress payments, or a contractor's failure to maintain the required contractor's license.

Termination clauses typically require a series of termination notices, allowing a grace period during which the noticed party can cure the default. It cannot be emphasized enough that initiating termination for default is a serious matter. Improper compliance with the notice provisions for termination could result in the public agency becoming the defaulting party.

Lastly, the **arbitration clause** of a contract may require some type of notice. The procedures for triggering arbitration are normally contained in the arbitration clause. Failure to initiate arbitration means the architect's decision becomes binding on matters of dispute between the public agency and the contractor. See Section 15.2 following for further discussion regarding arbitration.

§14.2 STATUTORY NOTICE REQUIREMENTS

In addition to the notice requirements provided in the contract itself, the State Contracting Act,[356] the Contract Code, the California Civil Code, and the California Code of Civil Procedure set forth notice and filing requirements needed to preserve the validity of the contractor's claim. The procedures outlined pertain to bond claims, stop notice rights, and mechanics' lien rights if private property is involved. See below for further discussion regarding applicable statutory provisions.

§ 14.3 OTHER PUBLIC WORKS STATUTES

Other California codes contain requirements for filing claims on public works projects. One of the few provisions that relate to all public agencies — state or local — is Contract Code § 9201, which empowers each public entity to "compromise or otherwise settle any claim relating to a contract at any time." Other than § 9201, the contracting rules for the various local agencies differ significantly from those for state contracts.

The State Contracts Act generally requires arbitration for disputes once the administrative remedies provided in the contract have been exhausted.[357] The existence of a clause for administrative remedies again points out the importance of a detailed analysis of all notice clauses in the contract. The arbitration generally must be commenced within 180 days of the final written decision by the state agency on the claim. Excepted from this time limit are issues regarding audit, latent defect, warranty, or guaranty claims.

The Contract Code has a separate chapter that must be consulted for guidance for each kind of local agency. To promote uniformity, the local public agency can adopt arbitration provisions used by the state.[358] In addition, it is recommended that a claim be made against the local agency under Gov't. Code § 910, *et seq.*

§ 14.4 ADDITIONAL STATUTES OF LIMITATIONS

The California Code of Civil Procedure contains a number of additional limitation periods for filing various types of lawsuits by or against construction contractors. Listed below are the more frequently encountered statutes of limitations.

California Statutes of Limitations (partial list)

10 years	Latent Defects (CCP 337.15)
4 years	Patent Defects (CCP 337.1)
4 years	Breach of Written Contract (CCP 337)

4 years   Rescind Written Contract (CCP 337(3))

3 years   Relief from Fraud or Mistake (CCP 338)

3 years   Damage to Real Property

2 years   Breach of Oral Contract (CCP 339)

1 year   Personal Injury

<u>Nelson v. Gorian & Associates</u>, 61 Cal App 4th 93 (1998), held that Code of Civil Procedure §337.15 (10 year statute of limitation for latent defects) begins to run as a bar on an action for soils subsidence when the work of improvement, i.e., the grading of the **specific lot**, was finished, as opposed to a notice of completion for the entire tract.

§ 14.5 TORT CLAIMS ISSUES

Contractors filing a tort claim on a public works project must comply with Government Code §§ 900-996.6, which govern claims procedures against public entities. An action involving a contract with a state agency must be filed within the time period, as specified in Contract Code §§ 19100.[359]

It is strongly recommended that a timely **government claim** be filed whenever a contractor seeks relief beyond the normal change order process or when negotiations stall. As a technical matter, the Contract Code provides that a Government Code claim need not be filed on a state contract claim as long as the Contract Code claim requirements are fulfilled.[360] However, in <u>Schaefer Dixon Associates v. Santa Ana Watershed Project Authority</u> (1996) 48 Cal. App.4th 524, the court found that a government claim was required and barred the claim as untimely. Since the Contract Code focuses on contract claims rather than the tort claims covered by the Government Code, and since many construction claims involve tort claims as well, it is appropriate to file a Gov't. Code § 900 *et seq.*, claim as a precaution. Again, the nature of the filing, to whom and when the claim is filed, and the appropriate strategy for claims submission are technical legal issues requiring a careful legal review.

Legal action on the claim must be commenced within six months after the final decision of the agency, the determination of rights by the hearing officer, or the accrual of the cause of action if there are no applicable claim procedures in the contract.[361]

A claim involving a contract with a local agency must amount to no more than $375,000 in order for Contract Code §§ 20104- 20104.6 to be applicable. The requirements for submission of a claim to a local agency are set forth in Pub. Contract Code §§ 20104.2. Public Contract Code §§ 20104.7, relating to contracting by local agencies, provides an action for damages by unsuccessful bidders as part of the competitive bidding process.

As discussed above, an unsuccessful bidder may have an action for damages against the local entity if the unsuccessful bidder suffered bid preparation or other damages resulting from its bid not being accepted.

The foregoing is not meant to be an all-inclusive list of applicable notice provisions or statutes of limitations; it is provided for illustrative purposes only. Each claim situation involves specific requirements.

Chapter 15

DISPUTE RESOLUTION

The Old Shasta County Courthouse, Redding
Courtesy University of California Library, Davis California

Summary:
When negotiation and compromise fail, some form of litigation may become necessary. This chapter lists the documents required for that litigation. Arbitration clauses are common in public works contracts (California Public Contracts Code Section 10240). Litigation and arbitration may be slow and expensive; mediation is a more cost and time effective procedure. Judicial arbitration may be required before a case can proceed to trial pursuant to CCP Section 1141.10-1141.3. Claims with an amount in controversy less than $50,000 per plaintiff generally require mandatory arbitration.

LITIGATION, ARBITRATION, MEDIATION, AND JUDICIAL ARBITRATION

If a claim or dispute cannot be resolved or wins the three phase approval discussed in Chapter 13, then some form of litigation may be necessary, as outlined below.

§ 15.1 LITIGATION

Most everyone would agree it is in the best interest of all the parties involved in a public works contract dispute to settle their differences through negotiations and compromise and to avoid litigation. However, if litigation is necessary, documentary evidence is very important. The key documents generated during a project are contracts, plans, specifications, revisions, bids, progress payment requests, detailed job costs reports, change order forms, schedules, daily reports, correspondence, and testing reports. Because of the complicated nature of construction, it is essential to present the claim in a manner that both the court and the jury can understand.

Construction litigation involves the same familiar stages as any other type of litigation: discovery, pretrial motions, trial, post-trial motions, and appeal.

§ 15.2 ARBITRATION

A public works contract may provide an arbitration clause, whereby the parties agree to resolve potential disputes by means of an arbitrator. Public Contract Code § 10240 provides that all claims by the State Contracts Act are subject to arbitration.[362]

Many form agreements require arbitration according to the American Arbitration Association guidelines (some require mediation, see below). An agreement to arbitrate may be made either in advance of a dispute (*e.g.*, in the contract) or after the dispute has arisen.[363] The California Arbitration Act[364] and the Federal Arbitration Act[365] enforce arbitration provisions in contracts. California courts and public policy favor the resolution of commercial disputes through arbitration "to promote judicial economy, and to settle disputes quickly and fairly."[366] Thus, courts will generally enforce such contractual provisions.[367]

Construction disputes are often extremely complex, and because arbitration involves many of the same drawbacks as litigation, it may not be the best alternative. For example, arbitration can be slow and expensive. But there may be efficiencies, in part because discovery rules do not apply, proceedings are informal, and it is not necessary to follow formal rules of evidence.[368]

If the claim is governed by the Contract Act, Contract Code § 10240.9 provides for joinder of any party who consents, and is necessary to avoid the risk of the joined party being subjected to inconsistent obligations or decisions.

Another consideration is whether the proceedings will be impacted by the arbitrator's expertise and/or possible bias. Having a better case based on the equities of the claim may appeal to the arbitrator's sense of fairness, resulting in a more favorable decision.

§ 15.3 MEDIATION

Parties to litigation often turn to other expedient forms of resolving disputes in an effort to avoid the high cost of litigation or arbitration. One such method is mediation.

The parties may decide to resolve their dispute by way of private mediation. The parties agree to employ a private mediator who assists and facilitates negotiations or settlement of a dispute in an informal manner. The mediator typically identifies the strengths and weaknesses in each party's case and attempts to find a fair resolution of the dispute.

§ 15.4 JUDICIAL ARBITRATION

Judicial arbitration is different from contractual arbitration discussed in item 2 above. Judicial arbitration is governed by Civil Procedures Code §§ 1141.10 - 1141.3, which provides that a case may be required to go to arbitration before it can proceed to trial. Mandatory submission applies to all at-issue civil cases in a superior court with more than 10 judges if, in the opinion of the court, the amount in controversy will not exceed $50,000 for each plaintiff.[369]

Chapter 16

SECRETS OF SUCCESSFUL PROJECTS

Santa Clara County Courthouse, San Jose
Photo by Robert Brekke

Summary:
This chapter contains guidelines for successful projects. These rules include: write good contracts and keep good records; consider hiring a clerk of works; be honest and direct in the handling of all of your problems. Select high quality projects and insure for all major risks. Train construction personnel well (they should all be familiar with basic claim requirements), don't be afraid to ask for help, and lastly, know that good advice is valuable commodity in a construction project.

It is no secret that successful construction projects require preparation, hard work and ingenuity, but there are common elements to successful projects. Twenty years of construction litigation experience, including the resolution of 2500 construction claims, are distilled in the following common sense approaches to projects. I only call them "secrets" since they seem to be unknown to many contractors seeking claims and/or owners faced with a claim:

Write good contracts. Know their contents. Avoid contracts that are overly oppressive. As a contractor and owner, seek to **disclaim consequential damages**, obtain a global limit of liability, limit indemnities to the amounts recoverable from insurance, limit remedies to repair or replacement within one year of installation, and be sure the scope of work and schedule are fixed. And when a problem occurs, **enforce** your contract rights

Handle problems promptly. It is easy to pretend the problem will go away. But you can not afford to ignore the problem. It is like an avalanche – it will get much worse unless it is stopped. Proper notice and documentation of the claim are immediate priorities. Assign an internal record-keeper to a major claim event. Do not overload the project manager with yet another "task." Call in consultants. If they do not prove themselves, replace them with another team of experts. But most of all, realize that every day that passes will make the problem worse if it is not addressed.

Be honest and direct. The most important project attribute is an iron clad reputation for honesty. A project history or claim that contains falsehoods, exaggerations or faulty analysis will not survive the first day of a hearing. It is also important to maintain a business like approach. The direct statement that certain claim events substantially increased your costs, that you are documenting those expenses, and that you suggest several steps to mitigate the future impact of the problem will be your most powerful weapon later in court. More importantly, by refusing to alienate the client, you will not be creating an additional personal or psychological barrier to payment by their representative.

Do not prejudice your claim by failure to give prompt notice. As discussed in the text, the failure to give proper notice can prejudice the owner's and construction manager's ability to respond to your claim and mitigate the costs of your claim. As such, failure to give proper notice will result in rejection of the claim.

Keep records of the events and costs associated with a claim. It is a relatively simple effort to set up a job account for each significant claim on a project. Have your superintendents and foreman keep records of claim costs. If the contract requires it, submit daily labor sheets for the effort on extras. Submit all extra material costs and standby time, including rental expense. Be sure that additional charges are documented (e.g., extra charge for concrete trucks to standby due to access delay caused by the owner.) For owners and tenants, consider a "clerk of the works."

Insure the major risks. A catastrophic loss on a project, such as a fire, may not qualify as a claim. There may be no recourse against anyone in the event of a loss, other than applicable insurance. **Don't let major risks slip through the cracks**. Use a specialized broker. Insure to reasonable limits and do not accept overly restrictive policy exclusions (e.g., no subsidence liability coverage in a policy covering a grading contractor).

Select the best projects, consultants, contractors & subcontractors. Projects that are well funded and important will navigate through claims more easily. Look for repeat business and specialized areas of construction where expertise will be appreciated and financially rewarded. Be the best owner and contractor that you can be.

Keep good records. Set up administrative and field systems that automatically identify and document potential problems. Be systematic and methodical. The Job Cost Accounting System (contractor) or Job Trending System (Owner or CM) should be reviewed weekly to determine if any significant overruns are expected. Additional record keeping steps should be setup as soon as a potential claim situation is encountered. Be sure to make the records suitable for later admission in arbitration or trial.

Train your people. It is vital that field people recognize claim situations and report them to company management. While not every construction professional can write a claim, or evaluate a legal or scheduling argument, they must all be aware of the basic elements of a claim and the avenues and obstacles to obtaining payment for valid claims.

Yell for Help. The least expensive cost of a construction project is good advice. A claims consultant or experienced construction attorney can provide enormous assistance in resolving claims. One of their tools is legal research. Your claim situation is not unique. There is probably a case that defines what you need to do to get a recovery. The construction attorney can also interview and retain experts in any field, and their views are confidential, due to the attorney/client privilege and work-product protection. It is possible to call an expert on short notice, get telephone advice, and resolve a claim in a single day.

Again, while these may not seem like secrets, they are only recognized as vital by a few major contractors, who have typically enjoyed a long and profitable history.

Reference Footnotes

[1] *See* Chapter 8 regarding selecting and awarding a public works contract to the lowest possible bidder.

[2] *See* below and Chapter 5 for a much more detailed discussion of design-build contracts.

[3] *See* <u>Worcester v. Granger Bros., Inc.</u>, 19 Mass. App. Ct. 379, 474 N.E.2d 1151, 1152 n.3, *review denied*, 394 Mass. 1103, 477 N.E.2d 595 (1985).

[4] California Bus. and Prof. Code § 5500.

[5] California Bus. and Prof. Code § 5500.1.

[6] California Bus. and Prof. Code § 6701.

[7] California Bus. and Prof. Code § 6702.

[8] California Bus. and Prof. Code § 6702.2.

[9] California Bus. and Prof. Code § 7026.

[10] Id.

[11] A construction manager is used primarily on large projects.

[12] 57 Cal. Opinion. Atty. Gen. 421, 472 (1971).

[13] See AIA document B141 for owner responsibilities, as well.

[14] The bidding phase is crucial in the public works process. See Chapter 8 for a complete discussion of advertising requirements & award of a public works contract to the lowest responsible bidder.

[15] See Chapter 8 for further discussion of awarding the contract.

[16] See Chapter 8 for further discussion.

[17] This is true only in general law cities and counties and charter cities and counties that require competitive bidding.

[18] *See* Chapter 8.

[19] Public Contract Code § 10335

[20] Government Code § 4526.

[21] Government Contract Code § 4526.

[22] Title 21, California Code of Regulations, §§ 1301-1361.

[23] Contract Code § 6106.

[24] Contract Code § 6106(b).

[25] Contract Code § 6106(c).

[26] Contract Code § 6106(d).

[27] Gov't. Code § 4527.

[28] Gov't Code § 4527(a).

[29] Gov't Code § 4527(b).

[30] Gov't Code § 4528(a)(1).

[31] Gov't Code § 4528(a).

[32] Gov't Code § 4528(b).

[33] Gov't Code § 4529.

[34] Gov't Code § 4529.5.

[35] *See, e.g.*, Allied Properties v. John A. Blume & Associates, Engineers, 25 Cal. App. 3d 848, 102 Cal. Rptr. 259 (1972).

[36] Gagne v. Bertran, 43 Cal. 2d 481, 275 P. 2d (1954).

[37] Stuart v. Crestview Mutual Water Co., 34 Cal. App. 3d 802, 110 Cal. Rptr. 543 (1973); Del Mar Beach Club Owners Ass'n. v. Imperial Contracting Co., 123 Cal. App. 3d 898, 914, 176 Cal. Rptr. 886 (1981).

[38] Allied Properties v. John A. Blume & Associates, Engineers, 25 Cal. App. 3d 848, 102 Cal. Rptr. 259 (1972).

[39] Arkansas Rice Growers Cooperative Ass'n v. Alchemy Industries, Inc., 797 F.2d 565 (8th Cir. 1986) (applying California law).

[40] United States v. Spearin, 248 U.S. 132 (1918); Welch v. State of California, 139 Cal. App. 3d 546, 188 Cal. Rptr. 726 (1983).

[41] Davis v. Boscou, 72 Cal. App. 323, 237 P. 401 (1925).

[42] Huang v. Garner, 157 Cal. App. 3d 404, 414—415, 203 Cal. Rptr. 800 (1984), criticized by Morris v. Horton, 22 Cal. App. 4th 968.

[43] Paxton v. County of Alameda, 119 Cal. App. 2d 393, 406, 259 P.2d 934 (1953).

[44] Bus. & Prof. Code § 5536.1.

[45] Felix v. Zlotoff, 90 Cal. App. 3d 155, 153 Cal. Rptr. 301 (1979).

[46] Davis v. Boscou, 72 Cal. App. 323, 237 P. 401 (1925).

[47] Harris v. Central Union High School District, 45 Cal. App. 669, 188 P. 617 (1920).

[48] Martin v. McMahan, 95 Cal. App. 75, 271 P. 1114 (1928).

[49] Rousseau v. Cohn, 20 Cal. App. 469, 129 P. 618 (1912) (proposed builder); Rosenheim v. Howze, 179 Cal. 309, 176 P. 456 (1918) (builder's loan); Stevenson v. County of San Diego, 26 Cal. 2d 842, 161 P.2d 553 (1945) (assumption of federal government of project); also 152 P.2d 644.

[50] *See e.g.* Anshen & Allen v. Marin Land Co., 197 Cal. App. 2d 214, 17 Cal. Rptr. 42 (1961) (Architect was entitled to the contract rate applied to $267,330 in construction costs, although the original estimate was $60,000-$70,000; the owner authorized progressively increasing construction costs during the course of the contract).

[51] Bodmer v. Turnage, 105 Cal. App. 2d 475, 233 P.2d 157 (1951).

[52] Fitzhugh v. Mason, 2 Cal. App. 220, 83 P. 282 (1905).

[53] Monaco v. Peoples National Bldg. Inc., 114 Cal. App. 122, 299 P. 548 (1931).

[54] Opdyke & Butler v. Silver, 111 Cal. App. 2d 912, 245 P.2d 306 (1952).

[55] *See, e.g.*, Waldinger Corp. v. Ashbrook-Simon-Hartley, Inc., 564 F. Supp. 970 (C.D. Ill. 1983), where a designer's performance specifications were allegedly so restrictive that they were deemed restrictive and discriminatory, aff'd. in part and remanded in part, Waldinger Corp. v. CRS Group Engineers, Inc. v. Clark Dietz

Div., 775 F.2d 781 (7th Cir. 1985).

[56] Krieger v. J. E. Greiner Co., 282 Md. 50, 382 A.2d 1069 (1978).

[57] Caldwell v. Bechtel, Inc., 631 F.2d 989 (D.C. Cir. 1980).

[58] Phillips v. United Engineer and Constructor, Inc., 600 N.E. 2d 1263 (Ind. App. 1992); also 235 Ill. App. 3d 5.

[59] Bus. & Prof. Code § 5536.25(c).

[60] U.S. use of Los Angeles Testing Laboratory v. Rogers & Rogers, 161 F. Supp. 132 (D. Cal. 1958).

[61] Bus. & Prof. Code § 5536.25(c).

[62] American-Hawaiian Engineering & Construction Co. v. Butler, 165 Cal. 497, 504, 133 P. 280 (1913).

[63] Palmer v. Brown, 127 Cal. App. 2d 44, 273 P.2d 306 (1954).

[64] Lundgren v. Freeman, 307 F.2d 104 (9th Cir. 1962), criticized by Sefton v. Pasadena Waldorf School, 219 Cal. App. 3d 359.

[65] Huber, Hunt & Nichols, Inc. v. Moore, 67 Cal. App. 3d 278, 299-301, 136 Cal. Rptr. 603 (1977), citing Lundgren v. Freeman, 307 F.2d 104 (9th Cir. 1962).

[66] Goldberg v. Underhill, 95 Cal. App. 2d 700, 213 P. 2d 516 (1950); Edward Barron Estate Co. v. Woodruff Co., 163 Cal. 561, 126 P. 351 (1912).

[67] Benenato v. McDougall, 166 Cal. 405, 137 P. 8 (1913).

[68] 17 U.S.C. §§ 101–103, 106, 120.

[69] See Chapter 6.

[70] Restatement (Second) of Contracts §§ 251 and 252 (1981).

[71] Barris v. Atlas Rock Co., 118 Cal. App., 606, 610, 5 P.2d 670 (1931).

[72] See Code of Civ. Proc. § 337 (four years of fraud actions); § 340 (one year for tort actions).

[73] Civ. Proc. Code § 342, referring to Government Code § 945.6.

[74] Civ. Proc. Code § 340.2.

[75] Civ. Proc. Code §§ 337.1 and 337.15.

[76] Industrial Risk Insurers v. Rust Engineering Co., 232 Cal. App. 3d 1038, 283 Cal. Rptr. 873 (1991).

[77] Regents of Univ. of Cal. v. Hartford Acc. and Indemnity Co., 21 Cal 3d 624, 147 Cal. Rptr. 486 (1978) (exclusion of sureties from scope of statute upheld); also 581 P.2d 197, superseded by statute as stated in Schwetz v. Minnerly, 220 Cal. App. 3d 296; Eden v. Van Tine, 83 Cal. App. 3d 879, 148 Cal. Rptr. 215 (1978) (exclusion of owners, tenants, and others in possession), superseded by statute as stated in Nelson v. Gorian, 61 Cal. App. 4th 93; and Barnhouse v. City of Pinole, 133 Cal. App. 3d 171, 183 Cal. Rptr. 881 (1982) (exclusion of materialman and suppliers.)

[78] See Appendix for AIA, Greenbook, and CalTrans standard general conditions.

[79] *See* Brown v. Sebastopol, 153 Cal. 704, 709, 96 P. 363 (1908); M. F. Kemper Construction Co. v. Los Angeles, 37 Cal. 2d 696, 704, 235 P. 2d 7 (1951); Hensler

v. Los Angeles, 124 Cal. App. 2d 71, 78, 268 P. 2d 12 (1954).

80 Civ. Code § 1856.

81 Contract Code § 7101.

82 Contract Code § 7102; See Mcguire & Hester v. San Francisco, 113 Cal. App. 2d 186, 247 P.2d 934 (1952); also see Milovich v. Los Angeles, 42 Cal. App. 2d 364, 108 P.2d 960 (1941); but see K & F Construction v. Los Angeles City Unified School Dist., 123 Cal. App. 3d 1063, 176 Cal. Rptr. 842 (1981).

83 Contract Code § 7100.

84 Contract Code § 7102; see McGuire & Hester v. San Francisco, 113 Cal. App. 2d 186, 247 P.2d 934 (1952); also see Milovich v. Los Angeles, 42 Cal. App. 2d 364, 108 P.2d 960 (1941); but see K & F Construction v. Los Angeles City Unified School Dist., 123 Cal. App. 3d 1063, 176 Cal. Rptr. 842 (1981).

85 Contract Code § 7105

86 Wm. R. Clarke Corp. v. Safeco Ins. Co., 15 Cal. 4th 882, 64 Cal. Rptr. 2d 578 (1997).

87 Superior Court of Los Angeles County, Nos. BC046221, BC027587, and BC052675, David P. Yaffe, Judge.

88 Second Dist., Div. One, Nos. B077931, BO78686, B081092, B082264.

89 Wm. R. Clarke Corp v. Safeco Ins. Co., 15 Cal. 4th 882, page 883.

90 Civil Code § 3262.

91 Civil Code § 3247.

92 See Chapter 6 for further discussion of insurance program.

93 See Chapter 7 for a more detailed discussion.

94 See Chapter 8 for a more detailed discussion of this area.

95 Lab. Code § 1771.

96 See e.g., Public Contract Code § 10227 and § 20136.

97 Civil Proc. Code § 337.

98 Civ. Code § 2782.

99 Civ. Code § 1717.

100 See, e.g., Contract Code § 10221-10224 (state contracting); Contract Code § 20426 (local contracting); see also, Liability Section, infra.

101 Contractors Labor Pool, Inc. v. Westway Contractors, Inc., 53 Cal. App. 4th 152, 61 Cal. Rptr. 2d 715 (1997). View This Case Only, Cases citing this case [No. B091490.Second Dist., Div. Three. February 28, 1997.] Contractors Labor Pool, Inc.,Plaintiff and Appellant, v. Westway Contractors, Inc. et al., Defendants and Respondents; American Bonding Co., Defendant and Appellant.

102 Superior Court of Los Angeles county, No. BC086794, Robert W. Parkin, Judge.

103 Opinion by Croskey, J., with Klein, P.J., and Kitching, J., concurring. [Contractors Labor Pool Inc. v. Westway Contractors, Inc., 53 Cal. App. 4th 152, page 153].

104 40 U.S.C. § 270 (1969).

105 This approach was discussed briefly in Chapter 2.

[106]Government Code § 5956, effective January 1, 1997.

[107]Government Code § 5956.3.

[108]Government Code § 5956.4.

[109]December 16, 1994.

[110]*See* Contract Code §§ 10180 and 20672 for state contract statutes. *See also* Contract Code §§ 20161-20162, which requires cities (except chartered cities) to put public projects out to bid.

[111]*See* Government Code § 4525 et. al.

[112]Government Code §§ 6508-6509; *See* Beckwith v. County of Stanislaus, 175 Cal. App. 2d 40, 345 P.2d 363 (1959).

[113]*See* Government Code § 14016.

[114]Contract Code §§ 10122, 10122.6; 21 C.C.R. § 1330; Los Angeles Dredging Co. v. Long Beach, 210 Cal. 348, 291 P. 839 (1930).

[115]*See* Government Code §§ 4525-4525.9; 21 C.C.R. §§ 1301, 1312, 1315.

[116]See Graydon v. Pasadena Redevelopment Agency, 104 Cal. App. 3d 631, 164 Cal. Rptr. 56 (1980).

[117]A.B.680 (1989-1900 Sess.), Stats. 1989, ch. 107 pp. 1017-1019, eff. July 10, 1989.

[118]Professional Engineers in California Government v. Department of Transportation, 13 Cal. App. 4th 585, 16 Cal. Rptr. 2d 599 (1993).

[119]A.B.680 (1989-1900 Sess.), Stats. 1989, ch. 107 pp. 1017-1019, eff. July 10, 1989.

[120]Professional Engineers in California Government v. Department of Transportation, 13 Cal. App. 4th 585, 16 Cal. Rptr. 2d 599 (1993).

[121]Contract Code § 100(d). *See* Graydon v. Pasadena Redevelopment Agency, 104 Cal. App. 3d 631, 164 Cal. Rptr. 56 (1980).

[122]Contract Code § 1100.

[123]Contract Code § 1101.

[124]Contract Code § 2000.

[125]Contract Code § 2050.

[126]Such efforts have been upheld by the U.S. Supreme Court where they are intended to remedy past discrimination. Richmond v. J.A. Croson Co., 488 U.S. 469, 109 S. Ct. 706 (1989).

[127]Contract Code § 3300.

[128]Contract Code § 3400.

[129]Contract Code § 3400(a).

[130]Contract Code §§ 4100-4114.

[131]Contract Code § 4100.

[132]Contract Code §§ 5100-5101.

[133]Contract Code §§ 6100-6107.

[134]Contract Code § 6101.

[135]Contract Code § 6107.

[136]Contract Code §§ 10100-10285.5.

[137]Contract Code § 10101.

[138]Contract Code § 10115.2. Other provisions regarding minority and women business participation goals for state contracts are set forth in Contract Code §§ 10115.33—10115.15.

[139]Domar Electric, Inc. v. City of Los Angeles, 9 Cal. 4th 161, 36 Cal. Rptr. 2d 521 (1994).

[140]Domar Electric, Inc. v. City of Los Angeles, 9 Cal. 4th 161, 36 Cal. Rptr. 2d 521 (1994).

[141]Domar Electric, Inc. v. City of Los Angeles, 41 Cal App. 4th 810, 48 Cal. Rptr. 2d 822 (1995) [No. B073387. Second Dist., Div. One. Dec. 28, 1995].

[142]Superior Court of Los Angeles County, No. BS020805, Robert H. O'Brien, Judge.

[143]Domar Electric, Inc. v. City of Los Angeles, 41 Cal. App. 4th 810, 811 (1995).

[144]Opinion by Masterson, J., with Spencer, P.J., and Ortega, J., concurring.

[145]Code Civ. Proc., § 526a.

[146]Contract Code § 10122.

[147]Contract Code §§ 10140, 10141. This area is discussed in much more detail in Chapter 9.

[148]Contract Code § 10160.

[149]Contract Code § 10167.

[150]Contract Code § 10169.

[151]Contract Code §§ 10180-10185.

[152]Contract Code §§ 10221-10225.

[153]Contract Code § 10226.

[154]Contract Code § 10227.

[155]Contract Code §§ 10231-10233.

[156]Contract Code §§ 10240-10240.13.

[157]Contract Code §§ 10250-10265.

[158]Contract Code §§ 10500-10513.

[159]Contract Code §§ 10700-10874.

[160]Contract Code § 20100. *See also* Contract Code §§ 20102-20104.70, relating to general provisions of local contracting.

[161]Contract Code § 20106.

[162]Contract Code § 20107.

[163]Contract Code §§ 20110-20118.4.

[164]Irwin v. Manhattan Beach, 65 Cal. 2d 13, 51 Cal. Rptr. 881, 415 P.2d (1966).

[165]Contract Code §§ 20120-20145.

[166]Contract Code §§ 20150-20150.14.

[167]Contract Code §§ 20160-20174.

[168]Contract Code §§ 20190-22300.

[169]Redwood City v. Moore, 231 Cal. App. 2d 563, 42 Cal. Rptr. 72 (1965).

[170]*See, e.g.,* San Diego Service Authority for Freeway Emergencies v. Superior Court, 198 Cal. App. 3d 1466, 244 Cal. Rptr. 440 (1988).

[171]Committee of Seven Thousand v. Superior Court, 45 Cal. 3d 491, 247 Cal. Rptr. 362, 754 P. 2d 708 (1988).

[172]Piledrivers' Local Union v. City of Santa Monica, 151 Cal. App. 3d 509, 198 Cal. Rptr. 731 (1984).

[173]Government Code §§ 6250-6260.

[174]5 U.S.C. § 552.

[175]Government Code § 6253.

[176]Government Code § 6252.

[177]Government Code § 6254.

[178]Government Code § 6254.5.

[179]Government Code § 6254(b).

[180]Id.

[181]48 C.F.R. 36.

[182]10 U.S.C. § 631(a); 10 U.S.C. § 2301; 41 U.S.C. § 252(b).

[183]Contract Code § 2000.

[184]Rules of Professional Conduct 2-100(a). This rule states that "while representing a client, a member shall not communicate directly or indirectly about the subject of the representation with a party the member knows to be represented by another lawyer in the matter, unless the lawyer has the consent of the other lawyer."

[185]Rules of Professional Conduct 2-100(c)(1); *See generally,* In the Matter of Riley (Review Dept. 1994) 3 Cal. State Bar Ct. Rptr. 91.

[186]This and other AIA documents are more fully explored in Chapter 6.

[187]Glenfed Development Corp. v. Superior Court, 53 Cal. App. 4th 1113, 62 Cal. Rptr. 2d 195 [No. B108546. Second Dist., Div. One. Mar. 27, 1997.]

[188]Superior Court of Los Angeles County, No. BC131389, Frances Rothschild, Judge.

[189]Code Civ. Proc. § 2031, subd. (1).

[190]Ins. Code § 790.03, subd. (h)(3).

[191]Opinion by Vogel (Miriam A.), J., with Ortega, Acting P.J., and Masterson, J., concurring. [Glenfed Development Corp. v. Superior Court, 53 Cal. App. 4th 1113, (1997).]

[192]Superior Court of Los Angeles County, No. BC023655, David Eagleson, temporary Judge, and William Burby, Judge.

[193]Cates Construction, Inc. v. Talbot Partners, 53 Cal. App. 4th 1420, 1421(1997).

[194]Opinion by Armstrong, J., with Turner, P.J., and Godoy Perez, J., concurring.

[195]Hydrotech Systems, Ltd. v. Oasis Waterpark, 52 Cal. 3d 988, 995 (1991).

[196]Asdourian v. Araj, 38 Cal. 3d 276, 211 Cal. Rptr. 703 (1985); 277 Cal. Rptr. 517, 803 P. 2d 370, 696 P. 2d 95.

[197]Executive Landscape Corp. v. San Vicente Country Villas IV Association, 145 Cal. App. 3d 496 (1983).

[198]Fillmore v. Irvine, 146 Cal. App. 3d 649, 194 Cal. Rptr. 319 (1983).

[199]Leonard v. Hermreck, 168 Cal. App. 2d 142 (1959).

[200]People v. Vis, 243 Cal. App. 2d 549 (1966).

[201]Contract Code § 3300(a).

[202]Id.

[203]Id. For an example of language used in public contract bidding documents, *see* City Council of Beverly Hills v. Superior Court of Los Angeles County, 272 Cal. App. 2d 876, 77 Cal. Rptr. (1969).

[204]Contract Code § 10164.

[205]Id.

[206]Bus. & Prof. Code § 7055.

[207]Bus. & Prof. Code § 7056.

[208]Bus. & Prof. Code § 7057.

[209]Bus. & Prof. Code § 7058.

[210]Bus. & Prof. Code § 7065.

[211]Bus. & Prof. Code § 7056. With regard to airports, a fair interpretation is that the contractor for terminal buildings should be a B licensed contractor.

[212]Bus. & Prof. Code § 7057.

[213]Id.

[214]Bus. & Prof. Code § 7058.

[215]Davies v. Contractors' State License Board, 79 Cal. App. 3d 940, 145 Cal. Rptr. 284 (1978).

[216]Bus. & Prof. Code § 7068.

[217]Bus. & Prof. Code § 7068.2.

[218]Bus. & Prof. Code § 7029.

[219]Id.

[220]Bus. & Prof. Code §§ 7029, 7076.

[221]Bus. & Prof. Code § 7029.1.

[222]Bus. & Prof. Code § 7031(a).

[223]Hydrotech Systems Ltd. v. Oasis Waterpark, 52 Cal. 3d 988 (1991).

[224]Id. at 997.

[225]Id.

[226]Bus. & Prof. Code § 7031(d).

[227]G.E. Hetrick & Associates, Inc. v. Summit Constr. & Maintenance Co., 11 Cal. App. 4th 318 (1992).

[228]Comet Theatre Enterprises, Inc. v. Cartwright, 195 F.2d 80, (9th Cir. Cal. 1952).

[229]American Sheet Metal, Inc. v. Em-Kay Engineering Co., 478 F. Supp. 809 (E.D. Cal. 1979).

[230]S & Q Constr. Co. v. Palma Ceia Dev. Organization, 179 Cal. App. 2d 364 (1960); Marshall v. Von Zumwalt, 120 Cal. App. 2d 807, 3 Cal. Rptr. 690 (1953).

[231]Construction Financial v. Perlite Plastering Co., 53 Cal. App. 4th 170, 61 Cal. Rptr. 2d 574 [No. B101077. Second Dist., Div. Three. Feb. 28, 1997].

[232](Bus. & Prof. Code § 7000, et seq.). (Superior Court of Los Angeles County, No. BC095313, Dzintra I. Janavs, Judge.)

[233]These various exemptions are contained in Bus. & Prof. Code §§ 7040-7054.5.

[234]Bus. & Prof. Code § 7045.

[235]Id.

[236]King v. Hinderstein, 122 Cal. App. 3d 430 (1981).

[237]Walker v. Thornsberry, 97 Cal. App. 3d 842, 158 Cal. Rptr. 862 (1979).

[238]Id.

[239]Bus. & Prof. Code § 7044(a).

[240]Bus. & Prof. Code § 7051.

[241]Ranchwood Communities Limited Partnership v. Jim Beat Construction Co., 49 Cal. App. 4th 1397, 57 Cal. Rptr. 2d 386 [No. D022053 Fourth Dist., Div. One. Oct. 8, 1996] [Reversed by Court of appeal].

[242]Superior Court of San Diego County, Nos. 660021 and 667861, Kevin W. Midlam, Judge.

[243]Ranchwood Communities Limited Partnership v. Jim Beat Construction Co., 49 Cal. App. 4th 1397: 1398.

[244]Opinion by Huffman, J., with Benke, Acting P.J., concurring. Concurring and dissenting opinion by McIntyre, J.

[245]Contract Code § 100; Graydon v. Pasadena Redevelopment Agency, 104 Cal. App.3d 631, 164 Cal. Rptr. 56 (1980), *cert. denied* 449 U.S. 983, 66 L.Ed.2d 246, 101 Sup. Ct. 400, *rehearing denied,* Coldby v. Harris. (1981) 449 U.S. 1104, 66 L.Ed.2d 832, 101 Sup.Ct. 905 (1980).

[246]*See* Committee of Seven Thousand v. Superior Court, 45 Cal. 3d 491, 247 Cal. Rptr. 362 (1988).

[247]Menefee v. County of Fresno, 163 Cal. App. 3d 1175, 1178, 210 Cal. Rptr. 99 (1985).

[248]*See* Steelgard Inc. v. Jannsen, 171 Cal. App. 3d 79, 217 Cal. Rptr. 152 (1985).

[249]*See, e.g.*, Contract Code §§ 20121 and 20150.4.

[250]*See* Gov't. Code §§ 4525 and14825.

[251]Los Angeles Dredging Co. v. Long Beach, 210 Cal. 348, 291 Cal. 348, 291 P. 839 (1930); Hiller v. City of Los Angeles, 197 Cal. App. 2d 685, 17 Cal. Rptr. 579 (1961); Constr. Indus. Force Account Council v. Delta Wetlands, 2 Cal. App. 4th 1589, 1594, 4 Cal. Rptr. 2d 43 (1992).

[252]See Los Angeles Dredging, supra.

[253]See Contract Code § 10140, state agency contracting.

[254]See Miller v. McKinnon, 20 Cal. 2d. 83, 124 P.2d 34 (1942).

[255]See Universal By-Products, Inc. v. Modesto, 43 Cal. App. 3d 145, 152, 117 Cal. Rptr. 525 (1974).

[256]Taylor Bus Serv. Inc. v. San Diego Bd. of Educ., 195 Cal. App. 3d 1331, 1341, 241 Cal. Rptr. 379 (1987).

[257]Menefee v. County of Fresno, 163 Cal. App. 3d 1175, 210 Cal. Rptr. 99 (1985) illustrates the application of the rules governing bid responsiveness for public works contracts.

[258]See Leo Michuda & Son Company v. Metropolitan Sanitary Dist., 97 Ill. App. 3d 340, 422 N.E.2d 1078 (1981).

[259]See generally, Menefee v. County of Fresno, 163 Cal. App. 3d 1175, 1179-81, 210 Cal. Rptr. 99 (1985).

[260]Gilotti Const. Co. v. City of Richmond, 45 Cal. App. 4th 897, 53 Cal. Rptr. 2d 389 (1996). [No. A071235.First Dist., Div. Three. May 22, 1996.]

[261]Superior Court of Contra Costa County, No. C95-02871, Judith A Sanders, temporary Judge.

[262]Taylor Bus Serv., Inc. v. San Diego Bd. of Education, 195 Cal. App. 3d 1331, 1341, 241 Cal. Rptr. 379 (1987).

[263]Inglewood - Los Angeles County Civic Center Authority v. Superior Court of Los Angeles County, 7 Cal. 3d 861, 103 Cal. Rptr. 689 (1972).

[264]Inglewood - Los Angeles County Civic Center Authority v. Superior Court of Los Angeles County, 7 Cal. 3d 861, 103 Cal. Rptr. 689 (1972); Boydston v. Napa Sanitation Dist., 222 Cal. App. 3d 1362, 272 Cal. Rptr. 458 (1990).

[265]R & A Vending Services, Inc. v. City of Los Angeles, 172 Cal. App. 3d 1188, 218 Cal. Rptr. 667 (1985).

[266]City of Inglewood - L.A. County Civic Center Authority v. Superior Court of Los Angeles, 7 Cal. 3d 861, 103 Cal. Rptr. 689 (1972).

[267]Raymond v. Fresno City Unified School Dist., 123 Cal. App. 2d 626, 267 P.2d 69 (1954).

[268]R & A Vending Services, Inc. v. City of Los Angeles, 172 Cal. App. 3d 1188, 218 Cal. Rptr. 667 (1985).

[269]See City of Inglewood supra; see also Taylor Bus Service, Inc. v. San Diego Bd. of Educ., 195 Cal. App. 3d 1331, 241 Cal. Rptr. 379 (1987).

[270]See, e.g., Contract Code § 10140 and § 22037; Gov't Code § 14825.

[271]See, e.g. Contract Code § 10141 and § 22037.

[272]7 Cal. 3d 861.

[273]*See* Officials Reject Contract Bids On Proof of Poor Safety Records, Wall St. Journal, Feb. 6, 1995, at B1.

[274]Business and Professional Code §§ 7000-7168.

[275]Hydrotech Systems v. Oasis Waterpark, 52 Cal. 3d 988, 995, 277 Cal. Rptr. 517 (1991); *also*, 803 P.2d. 370; *See also,* Bus. & Prof. Code §§ 7026-7026.2 for con tractor/builder definitions, which includes both subcontractors and specialty contractors.

[276]Bus. & Prof. Code § 7028.15.

[277]Bus. & Prof. Code § 7052.

[278]Bus. & Prof. Code § 10166.

[279]*See generally*, Baldwin-Lima-Hamilton Corp. v. Superior Court of San Francisco, 208 Cal. App. 2d 803, 25 Cal. Rptr. 798 (1962).

[280]Contract Code § 3400.

[281]*See* Contract Code § 10168.

[282]*See* Contract Code § 10167.

[283]*See* Contract Code § 10167.

[284]*See* Contract Code § 10167.

[285]*See* Contract Code § 10169.

[286]Contract Code § 5101.

[287]Contract Code § 5102.

[288]Contract Code § 5103; *See* A & A Electric, Inc. v. King, 54 Cal. App. 3d 457, 464, 126 Cal. Rptr. 585 (1976).

[289]*See, e.g.*, M. F. Kemper Constr. Co. v. Los Angeles, 37 Cal. 2d 696, 235 P.2d 7 (1951); Elsinore Union Sch. Dist. v. Kastorff, 54 Cal. 2d 380, 6 Cal. Rptr. 1 (1960); also, 353 P.2d 713; *but see*, Lemoge Electric v. County of San Mateo, 46 Cal. 2d 659, 297 P. 2d 638 (1956).

[290]Contract Code § 4100; Bay Cities Paving & Grading, Inc. v. Hensel Phelps Constr. Co., 56 Cal App. 3d 361, 128 Cal. Rptr. 632 (1976); Cal-Air Conditioning, Inc. v. Auburn Union School Dist., 21 Cal. App. 4th 655, 668, 26 Cal. Rptr. 2d 703 (1993).

[291]Contract Code § 4101.

[292]Contract Code § 4104.

[293]Contract Code § 4106.

[294]*See, e.g.,* Contract Code §§ 4110 and 4111.

[295]Contract Code § 4107.

[296]Contract Code § 4107.

[297]*See* Southern California Acoustics Co. v. C. V. Holder, Inc., 71 Cal. 2d 719, 79 Cal. Rptr. 319 (1969); *also* 456 P.2d 975; *See also*, Coast Pump Assoc. v. Stephen Tyler Corp., 62 Cal. App. 3d 421, 133 Cal. Rptr. 88 (1976) [REVERSED BY CT OF APPEAL!]; *But see* C. L. Smith Co. v. Roger Ducharme, Inc., 65 Cal. App. 3d 735, 135 Cal. Rptr. 483 (1977); Interior Systems, Inc., v. Del. E. Webb Corp., 121 Cal. App. 3d 312, 175 Cal. Rptr. 301 (1981).

[298]FTR International, Inc., Plaintiff and Appellant v. [NOT PUBLISHED] CITY OF PASADENA, Defendant and Respondent.

[299]Superior Court of Los Angeles County, No. BS036404, Robert H. O'Brien, Judge.

[300]FTR Internat., Inc. v. City of Pasadena, 53 Cal. App. 4th 634, Page 635 (1997); review denied May 14, 1997 with Reporter directed not to publish appellate opinion.

[301]Opinion by Woods, J., with Lillie, P.J., and Armstrong, J., *concurring.

[302]J & K Painting Co., Inc., Plaintiff and Appellant, v. Victoria L. Bradshaw, [Criticized by Bostanian v. Liberty Savings Bank, 52 Cal. App. 4th 1075 (1082)] as Labor Commissioner, etc., Defendant and Appellant(1996). 45 Cal.App. 4th 1394, 53 Cal. Rptr. 2d 496 No. A067893.First Dist., Div. Two. May 30, 1996].

[303]Superior Court of the City and County of San Francisco, No. 958810, Stuart R. Pollak, Judge.

[304]Opinion by Kline, P.J., with Phelan, J., * and Haerle, J., concurring. J & K Painting Co. v. Bradshaw, 45 Cal. App. 4th 1394, page 1395 (1996).

[305]Department of Industrial Relations v. Seaboard Surety Co., 50 Cal. App. 4th 1501, 58 Cal. Rptr. 2d 532 [No. D024620. Fourth Dist., Div. One. Nov. 21, 1996].

[306]Lab. Code §§ 96.7, 98.3, subd. (a).

[307]Lab. Code, §§ 1771 and 1774.

[308]Superior Court of San Diego County, No. 682725, Sheridan E. Reed, Judge.

[309]Department of Industrial Relations v. Nielsen Construction Co., 51 Cal. App. 4th 1016, 59 Cal. Rptr. 2d 785 [No. D024612. Fourth Dist., Div. One. Dec. 18, 1996].

[310]29 U.S.C. 1001 et seq.

[311]Superior Court of San Diego County, No. 681931, Arthur W. Jones, Judge.

[312]Department of Industrial Relations v. Nielsen Construction Co., 51 Cal. App.4th, page 1017.

[313]Opinion by Haller, J., with Kremer, P. J., and McIntyre, J., concurring.

[314]For example, special rules apply to the University of California.

[315]See Contract Code § 10180.

[316]See, e.g., Swinerton & Walberg Co. v. Inglewood - Los Angeles County Civic Center Authority, 40 Cal. App. 3d 98, 103-04, 114 Cal. Rptr. 834 (1974). [CT OF APPEAL REVERSED.]

[317]See, e.g., Baldwin-Lima-Hamilton Corp. v. Superior Court of San Francisco, 208 Cal. App. 2d 803, 25 Cal. Rptr. 798 (1962).

[318]Charles L. Harney, Inc. v. Durkee, 107 Cal. App. 2d 570, 237 P.2d 561 (1951).

[319]Raymond v. Fresno City Unified School Dist., 123 Cal. App. 2d 626, 267 P.2d 69 (1954).

[320]See Taylor Bus. Serv., Inc. v. San Diego Bd. of Educ., 195 Cal. App. 3d 1331, 241 Cal. Rptr. 379 (1987).

[321]See Supra.

[322]See generally, R & A Vending Services, Inc. v. City of Los Angeles, 172 Cal. App. 3d 1188, 218 Cal. Rptr. 667 (1985).

[323]*See generally,* State of Colorado v. Western Paving Construction Co., 630 F. Supp. 206 (1986). [REVERSED (833 F.2D 867) AND CRITICIZED (71 F.3D 119).]

[324]J.A. Croson Company v. City of Richmond, 822 F.2d 1355 (4th Cir. 1987) *quoting* Wygant v. Jackson Board of Education, 106 S. Ct. 1842 (1986). [CRITICIZED 920 F.2D 752.]

[325]*See* J. Edinger & Son, Inc. v. City of Louisville, Kentucky, 820 F.2d 213 (7th Cir. 1987).

[326]Associated General Contractors, Inc. v. San Francisco, 813 F.2d 922 (9th Cir. 1987). [CRITICIZED (1 F.3d 390) AND QUESTIONED (941 F.2d 910)].

[327]City of Inglewood - L.A. County Civic Center Authority v. Superior Court of Los Angeles, 7 Cal. 3d 861, 103 Cal. Rptr. 689 (1972).

[328]*See* Public Contract Code § 2000.

[329]Domar Electric, Inc. v. City of Los Angeles, 9 Cal. 4th 161, 36 Cal. Rptr. 2d 521 (1994). [SUPREME CT REVERSED JUDGMENT OF CT OF APPEALS.]

[330]*See* AIA Form A201.

[331]*See e.g.,* Contract Code § 10251.

[332]*See e.g.,* Bares v. Portola, 124 Cal. App. 2d 813, 269 P.2d 239 (1954); Thomas Kelly & Sons, Inc. v. Los Angeles, 6 Cal. App. 2d 539, 45 P.2d 223 (1935).

[333]*See e.g.* Jasper Construction Inc. v. Foothill Junior College District, 91 Cal. App. 3d 1, 153 Cal. Rptr. 767 (1979). [CT OF APPEALS REVERSED.]

[334]Hensler v. City of Los Angeles, 124 Cal. App. 2d 71, 268 P.2d 12 (1954).

[335]COAC, Inc. v. Kennedy Engineers, 67 Cal. App. 3d 916, 136 Cal. Rptr. 890 (1977) [CT OF APPEALS REVERSED].

[336]Coleman Engineering Co. v. North American Aviation, 65 Cal. 2d 396, 55 Cal. Rptr. 1 (1966).

[337]*See also,* Contract Code §§ 10105, 10226 (ever construction contract whose cost exceeds $35,000 with the departments of Transportation, Water Resources, General Services, or Boating and Waterways must include a liquidated damages clause for the contractor's delay).

[338]Bowman v. Santa Clara County, 153 Cal. App. 2d 707, 315 P.2d 67 (1957).

[339]State of California D.O.T. v. Guy F. Atkinson Co., 187 Cal. App. 3d 25, 231 Cal Rptr. 382 (1986).

[340]General Insurance Co. v. Commerce Hyatt House, 5 Cal. App. 3d 460, 85 Cal. Rptr. 317 (1970).

[341]*See,* Contract Drafting *supra.*

[342]Contract Code § 20104.5 is the local agency prompt pay statue, which is identical to the requirements of Contract Code § 10261.5 .

[343]*See* Witkin, Contracts §§ 772 and 773.

[344]*See* Witkin, Contracts § 786.

[345]206 Ct. Cl. 533, 513 F. 2d 585 (1975).

[346]207 Ct. Cl. 349, 518 F. 2d 594 (1975).

[347]175 Ct. Cl. 518, 360 F. 2d 634 (1966).

[348]Civil Code § 3109; A.J. Setting Co. v. Trustees of California State University & Colleges, 119 Cal. App. 3d 374, 174 Cal. Rptr. 43 (1981). [CRITICIZED (4 CAL. APP. 4th 1355).]

[349]Civil Code § 3196.

[350]Cal-Pacific Materials Co. v. Redondo Beach City School District, 94 Cal. App. 3d 652, 156 Cal. Rptr. 590 (1979). [REVERSED BY CT. OF APPEAL.]

[351]Civil Code § 3247.

[352]Civil Code § 3248.

[353]Civil Code § 3098 or a later notice under Civil Code §§ 3252- - -3.

[354]Penal Code § 72.

[355]Government Code § 12651(a).

[356]Gov't. Code § 1000, et seq.

[357]See Contract Code § 10240, et seq.

[358]Contract Code § 22201.

[359]See also, Public Contract Code § 10265.

[360]See Contract Code §§ 10265 and 19100.

[361]See Contract Code § 19100.

[362]Also see, Public Contract Code § 22300.

[363]Code of Civil Procedure § 1281.

[364]Code of Civil Procedure § 1280, et seq.

[365]9 U.S.C. § 1 et seq.

[366]Garden Grove Community Church v. Pittsburgh-Des Moines Steel Co., 140 Cal. App. 3d 251, 263, 191 Cal. Rptr. 15 (1983). [REVERSED BY CT OF APPEAL.]

[367]Jones v. Kvistad, 19 Cal. App. 3d 836, 97 Cal. Rptr. 100 (1971).

[368]See Lesser Towers, Inc. v. Roscoe-Ajax Construction Co., 271 Cal. App. 2d 675, 677 n.1, 77 Cal. Rptr. 100, 102 n.1 (1969) (19 months arbitration costing $400,000 in arbitration expenditures, exclusive of attorneys' fees).

[369]Code of Civil Procedure § 1141.11.

About the Author

Ernest C. Brown, Esq., P.E.

Ernest C. Brown, Esq., P.E., founder of Ernest Brown & Company, is a leading California construction attorney, claims consultant, arbitrator, and mediator. Over the past twenty years, Mr. Brown has spoken at more than 250 seminars on construction law and regularly advises public agencies, general contractors, design firms, and other construction organizations regarding bidding, contracts, claims, and disputes on large construction projects.

He has been a legal advisor for numerous domestic and international construction projects, including the John Wayne Airport, Anaheim Arena, Orange County Performing Arts Center, Bay Area Rapid Transit (BART), the Los Angeles MTA, the Central Arizona Project, and many industrial, roadway, bridge, and sewage treatment projects. He was formerly Corporate Counsel with Fluor Daniel and a shareholder in a major California law firm.

Mr. Brown prepared the first edition of these materials for the California Continuing Education of the Bar Program on "Public Works: Contracts and Litigation" (May 1995). The program was attended by more than 600 California attorneys.

Academic:

Graduate of Massachusetts Institute of Technology (MIT) in Civil Engineering (1975) (Karl Taylor Compton Prize)

Master in Construction Management, University of California Berkeley (1978)

Juris Doctor – Law, University of California Berkeley (Boalt Hall – 1978) (Harmon Prize in Environmental Law & American Jurisprudence Award in Criminal Procedure)

Memberships:

The California Bar

American Bar Association, ABA Forum Committee for the Construction Industry

National Society of Professional Engineers

Legal Advisory Committee for the Associated General Contractors of California

GLOSSARY

Additional Services
Services which generally require additional compensation beyond fixed fee or lump sum price, as used in previous additions of AIA B-141 Owner - Architect Agreement.

Architect
A person who offers or performs "professional services which require the skills of an architect in the planning of sites, and the design, in whole or in part, of buildings, or groups of buildings and structures" is engaging in the practice of architecture. A person must be licensed to hold themselves out as an "architect" or as "practicing architecture" in the state of California.

Architect - Engineer Agreement
An agreement for the provision of engineering services to an architect, or visa versa.

Architect - Owner Agreement
An agreement for the provision of architectural services to an owner for a work of im-provement (e.g. AIA B-141).

Bar Charts
A simple chart consisting of bars that identify the starting and completion dates of par-ticular activities critical to a construction project.

Basic Services
Services which are included in the fixed-fee or lump sum structure of a services agree-ment. (e.g. AIA B 141).

Bid Shopping
The unethical substitution or browbeating by the general contractor of subcontractors after submission and acceptance of the bid by a public agency. There is generally no legal prohibition against bid shopping in private projects.

Bid Documents
The set of documents published by a public entity or private owner prior to the time of bid. These typically include an invitation to bid, the date, time, and place of submitting bids, the bidding form, the manner of requesting clarification prior to the bid, the date, time and location of any pre-bid meeting, the plans, specifications and proposed form of contract, and other requirements for the project.

Bid Peddling
A term equivalent to Bid Shopping, see above.

Change order
A contractually issued change in the scope or timing of the work, generally stating the additive or deductive monetary amount and any extension or decrease in the time of performance.

Competitive lump sum bidding
The traditional method of bidding where a group of contractors are asked to submit a lump sum, fixed price bid for a fixed scope of work, generally for performance within an agreed time period.

Construction Phase Services
The services provided by an architect or engineer during the construction of the project.

These may include observation and reporting on job progress, answering questions from the field or owner, inspection and testing, and change order management.

Construction manager
A person or entity hired by the owner to oversee the progress of the job. The responsibilities generally include monitoring the day-to-day on-site activities of the general contractor. The scope of construction management services vary widely from overall job responsibility (e.g. hiring architects, engineers, and general contractors) to more limited roles, such as providing on-site observation for the owner.

Contract documents
The group of documents that generally comprise the general contractor's entire scope of work, including but not limited to the contract, general conditions, special conditions, plans, specifications, and referenced specifications and standards.

Cost-plus contracts
A contract which provides reimbursement for all costs of the services or the construction, plus compensation for overhead and profit. The "plus" often takes the form of a percentage of the underlying costs of performance.

Critical path method (CPM)
Depicts the flow of time and work. It identifies the critical activities of the project and the durations of each activity, along with critical deadline dates.

Critical path
The series of linked activities that can not be delayed without the project duration being delayed as well. Other, non-essential activities can be delayed, for various durations, without the project being delayed. The amount of extra time allotted to the non-critical activities is referred to as "float".

Forward priced change order
An advance agreement on changes to minimize the volume of unsettled claims.

Damage for delay
Precludes recovery of damages by the contractor or subcontractor when the owner creates a contractually compensable delay.

Design-build
An arrangement by which the owner generally contracts with a single entity for design and construction of the project.

Design Builder
The arrangement that allows a single point of responsibility to the owner for both design and construction. It may involve: 1. A general contractor that employs its own architects or engineers or retains them on a consulting basis; or 2. a joint venture between a general contractor and a design firm. On rare occasions, the design-builder is an architecture or engineering firm that is also licensed as a general contractor and subcontracts the construction phase.

Design-bid-build
The traditional project delivery approach where bidding occurs after the entire project is designed, and the contract is thereafter awarded to a general contractor on typically a lump sum basis.

Differing site conditions clause
Typical clause that may give the contractor relief for time or costs associated with: Type I Underground conditions materially differing from those represented in the site geology reports; Type II Underground conditions substantially different than those generally encountered or expected in the area; or Type III Hazardous Waste or Asbestos. These types are contained in a variety of standardized construction contracts.

DVE – Disabled Veterans Enterprise.

Engineer
One who possesses education, training, and experience in engineering services, and has special knowledge in various areas, including design of public or private utilities.

Fast track
A project delivery approach which allows construction to begin before the final drawings are completed for a project. Generally used where time is of the essence to the owner, often resulting in design inefficiencies and cost escalations.

Fixed price contracts
A contract which the contractor agrees to complete a project for a fixed price according to the contract documents.

Force account
A public works term used to denote reimbursable work of a transitory or undefined scope. Generally limited to small amounts (e.g., $15,000).

General law cities
Those cities operating under the general law of California rather than under a city charter.

General law counties
Those counties operating under the general law of California rather than under a county charter.

General Contractor
A contractor licensed by the Department of Consumer Affairs, State Contractors Licence Board to act as a general contractor. The major classifications are "A," General Engineering Contractor; "B," Building Contractor; and "C," Speciality or subcontractor.

General Contractor Agreement
The main agreement between the owner and the general contractor.

Guaranteed maximum price
Typical provision of a reimbursable cost agreement where the owner wishes either an upper boundary on cost, or an authorization level where the contractor must return to the owner for further financial authorization.

Liquidation Agreement
An agreement which allows the general contractor to delay paying the subcontractors claim accounts until the claim is resolved with the owner.

Lowest responsible bidder
The bidder that submits the low bid and is capable of performing the work.

Responsive bidder
A bidder whose bid responds in accordance with the terms of the Invitation to Bid.

Lump sum contracts
Contracts with a single stipulated price, generally for a fixed scope of work. Lump sum contracts may also contain unit prices or other terms for extra or unanticipated work.

MBE - Minority Business Enterprise.

Mechanic's lien
A statutory lien against a real property interest (owned parcel, leasehold, or improvements) that is allowed in favor of improvers of real property. The terms for creating and enforcing mechanic's liens are strict and contain rigid timetables.

Multiple prime contracts
A set of independent prime contracts entered into by the owner for executing separate aspects of a project. These arrangements can cause problems if the owner does not adequately coordinate the work.

Negotiated price
A technique of contract award where the owner and contractor negotiate with regard to the price and scope of the work.

No bid decision
A business judgment by a contractor not to bid certain work because of perceived risks or present workload.

Owner
The party who will eventually own the completed work of improvement.

Paid-when-paid clause
A controversial clause in subcontracts that restricted payment to the subcontractor until after the general contractor was paid. Found invalid in California under Clark v. Safco, 15 Cal. 4th 882, (1997).

Payment bonds
A bond posted by a general contractor assuring payment of labor and materials on jobsites. (Also called Labor and Materials Bonds.)

Performance specifications
A method of contracting in which the architect or engineer sets forth criteria for performance that the vendor or contractor must meet. Common on large mechanical, electrical or power project systems.

Public works contract
An agreement for the erection, construction, alteration, repair or improvement of any public structure, building, road, or other public improvement of any kind.

Public entity
The state, county, city, city and county, district, public authority, public agency, municipal corporation, or any other public subdivision or public corporation in the state.

Public works
The work of improvement carried out by a public entity. The term is defined in various ways in the California Civil Code, Public Contracts Code and Government Code, depending upon the statute involved.

Punch list

A list of items yet to be completed under a construction contract. Often created at or after the time of substantial completion.

Reimbursable Cost Contract

A method of contracting in which the contractor is compensated for its actual costs (e.g. labor, materials and field overhead) and in addition, receives a stipulated payment for its other overheads and profit (e.g., percentage fee or fixed fee).

Release of claims clause

A fairly unusual contract clause that states that claims of the contractor are released unless asserted by a certain point in the job, such as submission of the final invoice.

Retention provisions

A customary type of clause by which a percentage of the contractor's invoice for competed work is retained by the owner until the completion of the work as a whole. Generally, retention is from 5% to 10% of the submitted invoice. It is generally released upon actual completion, although a portion may be released during the project if the contractor posts security, or upon certain milestones such as substantial completion.

Set-aside

A percentage of the project that is intended to be performed by a specific type of entity, such as a DME or MBE.

Shop drawings

Construction drawings submitted by the contractor to the owner and architect based upon the original plans and specifications.

Sole source

A provision that requires a specific material or piece of equipment be purchased from a specified vendor or manufacturer. In public works, a set procedure must generally be followed to allow this departure from customary competitive bidding and "or equal" provisions of the low bidder system.

Stop notices

A statutory technique that stops payments to the general contractor, generally to secure payment to the subcontractor or vendor.

Turnkey

A contracting approach by which a single entity design, procures, constructs and commissions a project, so that an owner need only "turn the key."

Unit-price contracts

A contract which involves a fixed price per unit of material or quantity of work to be performed.

Value Engineering clause

Provides extra compensation to a contractor for cost reduction changes in the plans or specifications.

WBE - Women Business Enterprises

TABLE OF CASES

A & A Electric, Inc. v. King, 54 Cal. App. 3d 457, 464, 126 Cal. Rptr. 585 (1976).

A.J. Setting Co. v. Trustees of California State University & Colleges, 119 Cal. App. 3d 374, 174 Cal. Rptr. 43 (1981). [CRITICIZED (4 CAL. APP. 4th 1355).]

Allied Properties v. John A. Blume & Associates, Engineers, 25 Cal. App. 3d 848, 102 Cal. Rptr. 259 (1972).

American Sheet Metal, Inc. v. Em-Kay Engineering Co., 478 F. Supp. 809 (E.D. Cal. 1979).

American-Hawaiian Engineering & Construction Co. v. Butler, 165 Cal. 497, 504, 133 P. 280 (1913).

Anshen & Allen v. Marin Land Co., 197 Cal. App. 2d 214, 17 Cal. Rptr. 42 (1961).

Arkansas Rice Growers Cooperative Ass'n v. Alchemy Industries, Inc., 797 F.2d 565 (8th Cir. 1986) (applying California law).

Asdourian v. Araj, 38 Cal. 3d 276, 211 Cal. Rptr. 703 (1985); 277 Cal. Rptr. 517, 803 P. 2d 370, 696 P. 2d 95.

Associated General Contractors, Inc. v. San Francisco, 813 F.2d 922 (9th Cir. 1987). [CRITICIZED (1 F.3d 390) AND QUESTIONED (941 F.2d 910)].

Baldwin-Lima-Hamilton Corp. v. Superior Court of San Francisco, 208 Cal. App. 2d 803, 25 Cal. Rptr. 798 (1962).

Bares v. Portola, 124 Cal. App. 2d 813, 269 P.2d 239 (1954).

Barris v. Atlas Rock Co., 118 Cal. App., 606, 610, 5 P.2d 670 (1931).

Bay Cities Paving & Grading, Inc. v. Hensel Phelps Constr. Co., 56 Cal App. 3d 361, 128 Cal. Rptr. 632 (1976).

Beckwith v. County of Stanislaus, 175 Cal. App. 2d 40, 345 P.2d 363 (1959).

Benenato v. McDougall, 166 Cal. 405, 137 P. 8 (1913).

Bodmer v. Turnage, 105 Cal. App. 2d 475, 233 P.2d 157 (1951).

Bowman v. Santa Clara County, 153 Cal. App. 2d 707, 315 P.2d 67 (1957).

Boydston v. Napa Sanitation Dist., 222 Cal. App. 3d 1362, 272 Cal. Rptr. 458 (1990).

Brown v. Sebastopol, 153 Cal. 704, 709, 96 P. 363 (1908).

Cal-Air Conditioning, Inc. v. Auburn Union School Dist., 21 Cal. App. 4th 655, 668, 26 Cal. Rptr. 2d 703 (1993).

Cal-Pacific Materials Co. v. Redondo Beach City School District, 94 Cal. App. 3d 652, 156 Cal. Rptr. 590 (1979). [REVERSED BY CT. OF APPEAL.]

Caldwell v. Bechtel, Inc., 631 F.2d 989 (D.C. Cir. 1980).

Cates Construction, Inc. v. Talbot Partners, 53 Cal. App. 4th 1420, 1421(1997).

Charles L. Harney, Inc. v. Durkee, 107 Cal. App. 2d 570, 237 P.2d 561 (1951).

City Council of Beverly Hills v. Superior Court of Los Angeles County, 272 Cal. App. 2d 876, 77 Cal. Rptr. (1969).

City of Inglewood - L.A. County Civic Center Authority v. Superior Court of Los Angeles, 7 Cal. 3d 861, 103 Cal. Rptr. 689 (1972).

COAC, Inc. v. Kennedy Engineers, 67 Cal. App. 3d 916, 136 Cal. Rptr. 890 (1977) [CT OF APPEALS REVERSED].

Coleman Engineering Co. v. North American Aviation, 65 Cal. 2d 396, 55 Cal. Rptr. 1 (1966).

Comet Theatre Enterprises, Inc. v. Cartwright, 195 F.2d 80, (9th Cir. Cal. 1952).

Committee of Seven Thousand v. Superior Court, 45 Cal. 3d 491, 247 Cal. Rptr. 362, 754 P. 2d 708 (1988).

Committee of Seven Thousand v. Superior Court, 45 Cal. 3d 491, 247 Cal. Rptr. 362 (1988).

Constr. Indus. Force Account Council v. Delta Wetlands, 2 Cal. App. 4th 1589, 1594, 4 Cal. Rptr. 2d 43 (1992).

Construction Financial v. Perlite Plastering Co., 53 Cal. App. 4th 170, 61 Cal. Rptr. 2d 574 [No. B101077 Second Dist., Div. Three. Feb. 28, 1997].

Contractors Labor Pool, Inc. v. Westway Contractors, Inc., 53 Cal. App. 4th 152, 61 Cal. Rptr. 2d 715 (1997). View This Case Only, Cases citing this case [No. B091490. Second Dist., Div. Three. February 28, 1997.] Contractors Labor Pool, Inc., Plaintiff and Appellant v. Westway Contractors, Inc. et al., Defendants and Respondents; American Bonding Co., Defendant and Appellant.

Contractors Labor Pool Inc. v. Westway Contractors, Inc., 53 Cal. App. 4th 152, page 153].

Davies v. Contractors' State License Board, 79 Cal. App. 3d 940, 145 Cal. Rptr. 284 (1978).

Davis v. Boscou, 72 Cal. App. 323, 237 P. 401 (1925).

Del Mar Beach Club Owners Ass'n.v. Imperial Contracting Co., 123 Cal. App. 3d 898, 914, 176 Cal. Rptr. 886 (1981).

Department of Industrial Relations v. Nielsen Construction Co., 51 Cal. App. 4th , page 1017.

Department of Industrial Relations v. Seaboard Surety Co., 50 Cal. App. 4th 1501, 58 Cal. Rptr. 2d 532 [No. D024620. Fourth Dist., Div. One. Nov. 21, 1996].

Department of Industrial Relations v. Nielsen Construction Co., 51 Cal. App. 4th 1016, 59 Cal. Rptr. 2d 785 [No. D024612. Fourth Dist., Div. One. Dec. 18, 1996].

Domar Electric, Inc. v. City of Los Angeles, 9 Cal. 4th 161, 36 Cal. Rptr. 2d 521 (1994). [SUPREME CT REVERSED JUDGMENT OF CT OF APPEALS.]

Dynalectron Corp. v. United States.

Edward Barron Estate Co. v. Woodruff Co., 163 Cal. 561, 126 P. 351 (1912).

Industrial Relations v. Seaboard Surety Co., 50 Cal. App. 4th 1501, 58 Cal. Rptr. 2d 532 [No. D024620.Fourth Dist., Div. One. Nov 21,1996] [REVERSED BY CT OF APPEAL].

Inglewood - Los Angeles County Civic Center Authority v. Superior Court of Los Angeles County, 7 Cal. 3d 861, 103 Cal. Rptr. 689 (1972).

Irwin v. Manhattan Beach, 65 Cal. 2d 13, 51 Cal. Rptr. 881, 415 P.2d (1966).

J & K Painting Co. v. Bradshaw, 45 Cal. App. 4th 1394, page 1395 (1996).

J & K Painting Co., Inc., Plaintiff and Appellant, v. Victoria L. Bradshaw, [Criticized by Bostanian v. Liberty Savings Bank, 52 Cal. App. 4th 1075 (1082)] as Labor Commissioner, etc., Defendant and Appellant(1996). 45 Cal.App. 4th 1394, 53 Cal. Rptr. 2d 496 No. A067893. First Dist., Div. Two. May 30, 1996].

J. Edinger & Son, Inc. v. City of Louisville, Kentucky, 820 F.2d 213 (7th Cir. 1987).

J.A. Croson Company v. City of Richmond, 822 F.2d 1355 (4th Cir. 1987) quoting Wygant v. Jackson Board of Education, 106 S. Ct. 1842 (1986). [CRITICIZED 920 F.2D 752.]

Jasper Construction Inc. v. Foothill Junior College District, 91 Cal. App. 3d 1, 153 Cal. Rptr. 767 (1979). [CT OF APPEALS REVERSED.]

Jones v. Kvistad, 19 Cal. App. 3d 836, 97 Cal. Rptr. 100 (1971).

K & F Construction v. Los Angeles City Unified School Dist., 123 Cal. App. 3d 1063, 176 Cal. Rptr. 842 (1981).

King v. Hinderstein, 122 Cal. App. 3d 430 (1981).

Krieger v. J. E. Greiner Co., 282 Md. 50, 382 A.2d 1069 (1978).

Lemoge Electric v. County of San Mateo, 46 Cal. 2d 659, 297 P. 2d 638 (1956).

Leo Michuda & Son Company v. Metropolitan Sanitary Dist., 97 Ill. App. 3d 340, 422 N.E.2d 1078 (1981).

Leonard v. Hermreck, 168 Cal. App. 2d 142 (1959).

Lesser Towers, Inc. v. Roscoe-Ajax Construction Co., 271 Cal. App. 2d 675, 677 n.1, 77 Cal. Rptr. 100, 102 n.1 (1969).

Los Angeles Dredging Co. v. Long Beach, 210 Cal. 348, 291 Cal. 348, 291 P. 839 (1930).

Lundgren v. Freeman, 307 F.2d 104 (9th Cir. 1962), criticized by Sefton v. Pasadena Waldorf School, 219 Cal. App. 3d 359.

M. F. Kemper Construction Co. v. Los Angeles, 37 Cal. 2d 696, 704, 235 P. 2d 7 (1951).

Marshall v. Von Zumwalt, 120 Cal. App. 2d 807, 3 Cal. Rptr. 690 (1953).

Martin v. McMahan, 95 Cal. App. 75, 271 P. 1114 (1928).

Mcguire & Hester v. San Francisco, 113 Cal. App. 2d 186, 247 P.2d 934 (1952).

Menefee v. County of Fresno, 163 Cal. App. 3d 1175, 1178, 210 Cal. Rptr. 99 (1985).

Menefee v. County of Fresno, 163 Cal. App. 3d 1175, 1179-81, 210 Cal. Rptr. 99 (1985).

Miller v. McKinnon, 20 Cal. 2d. 83, 124 P.2d 34 (1942).

Milovich v. Los Angeles, 42 Cal. App. 2d 364, 108 P.2d 960 (1941).

Monaco v. Peoples National Bldg. Inc., 114 Cal. App. 122, 299 P. 548 (1931).

Opdyke & Butler v. Silver, 111 Cal. App. 2d 912, 245 P.2d 306 (1952).

Opinion by Vogel (Miriam A.), J., with Ortega, Acting P.J., and Masterson, J., concurring. [Glenfed Development Corp. v. Superior Court, 53 Cal. App. 4th 1113, (1997).]

Palmer v. Brown, 127 Cal. App. 2d 44, 273 P.2d 306 (1954).

Paxton v. County of Alameda, 119 Cal. App. 2d 393, 406, 259 P. 2d 934 (1953).

People v. Vis, 243 Cal. App. 2d 549 (1966).

Phillips v. United Engineer and Constructor, Inc., 600 N.E. 2d 1263 (Ind. App. 1992); also 235 Ill. App. 3d 5.

Piledrivers' Local Union v. City of Santa Monica, 151 Cal. App. 3d 509, 198 Cal. Rptr. 731 (1984).

Professional Engineers in California Government v. Department of Transportation, 13 Cal. App. 4th 585, 16 Cal. Rptr. 2d 599 (1993).

R & A Vending Services, Inc. v. City of Los Angeles, 172 Cal. App. 3d 1188, 218 Cal. Rptr. 667 (1985).

Ranchwood Communities Limited Partnership v. Jim Beat Construction Co., 49 Cal. App. 4th 1397, 57 Cal. Rptr. 2d 386 [No. D022053 Fourth Dist., Div. One. Oct. 8, 1996] [Reversed by Court of appeal].

Raymond v. Fresno City Unified School Dist., 123 Cal. App. 2d 626, 267 P.2d 69 (1954).

Redwood City v. Moore, 231 Cal. App. 2d 563, 42 Cal. Rptr. 72 (1965).

Regents of Univ. of Cal. v. Hartford Acc. and Indemnity Co., 21 Cal 3d 624, 147 Cal. Rptr. 486 (1978) (exclusion of sureties from scope of statute upheld); also 581 P.2d 197, superseded by statute as stated in Schwetz v. Minnerly, 220 Cal. App. 3d 296; Eden v. Van Tine, 83 Cal. App. 3d 879, 148Cal. Rptr. 215 (1978) (exclusion of owners, tenants, and others in possession), superseded by statute as stated in Nelson v. Gorian, 61 Cal. App. 4th 93; and Barnhouse v. City of Pinole, 133 Cal. App. 3d 171, 183 Cal. Rptr. 881 (1982) (exclusion of materialman and suppliers).

Richmond v. J.A. Croson Co., 488 U.S. 469, 109 S. Ct. 706 (1989).

Rousseau v. Cohn, 20 Cal. App. 469, 129 P. 618 (1912) (proposed builder).

Rosenheim v. Howze, 179 Cal. 309, 176 P. 456 (1918) (builder's loan).

Stevenson v. County of San Diego, 26 Cal. 2d 842, 161 P.2d 553 (1945) (assumption of federal government of project); also 152 P.2d 644.

S & Q Constr. Co. v. Palma Ceia Dev. Organization, 179 Cal. App. 2d 364 (1960).

San Diego Service Authority for Freeway Emergencies v. Superior Court, 198 Cal. App. 3d 1466, 244 Cal. Rptr. 440 (1988).

Southern California Acoustics Co. v. C. V. Holder, Inc., 71 Cal. 2d 719, 79 Cal. Rptr. 319 (1969); also 456 P.2d 975; See also, Coast Pump Assoc. v. Stephen Tyler Corp., 62 Cal. App. 3d 421, 133 Cal. Rptr. 88 (1976) [REVERSED BY CT OF APPEAL!]; But see, C. L.

Smith Co. v. Roger Ducharme, Inc., 65 Cal. App. 3d 735, 135 Cal. Rptr. 483 (1977).

Interior Systems, Inc., v. Del. E. Webb Corp., 121 Cal. App. 3d 312, 175 Cal. Rptr. 301 (1981).

Stacy & Witebeck, Inc. v. City of San Francisco (1995) 36 Cal. App. 4th 1074, 44 Cal. Rptr. 2d 472 [REVERSED BY CT OF APPEAL].

State of Colorado v. Western Paving Construction Co., 630 F. Supp. 206 (1986). [REVERSED (833 F.2D 867) AND CRITICIZED (71 F.3D 119)].

State of California D.O.T. v. Guy F. Atkinson Co., 187 Cal. App. 3d 25, 231 Cal Rptr. 382 (1986).

Steelgard Inc. v. Jannsen, 171 Cal. App. 3d 79, 217 Cal. Rptr. 152 (1985).

Stuart v. Crestview Mutual Water Co., 34 Cal. App. 3d 802, 110 Cal. Rptr. 543 (1973).

Swinerton & Walberg Co. v. Inglewood - Los Angeles County Civic Center Authority, 40 Cal. App. 3d 98, 103-04, 114 Cal. Rptr. 834 (1974). [CT OF APPEAL REVERSED.]

Taylor Bus Serv., Inc. v. San Diego Bd. of Education, 195 Cal. App. 3d 1331, 1341, 241 Cal. Rptr. 379 (1987).

Thomas Kelly & Sons, Inc. v. Los Angeles, 6 Cal. App. 2d 539, 45 P.2d 223 (1935).

U.S. use of Los Angeles Testing Laboratory v. Rogers & Rogers, 161 F. Supp. 132 (D. Cal. 1958).

United States v. Spearin, 248 U.S. 132 (1918).

Universal By-Products, Inc. v. Modesto, 43 Cal. App. 3d 145, 152, 117 Cal. Rptr. 525 (1974).

Waldinger Corp. v. Ashbrook-Simon-Hartley, Inc., 564 F. Supp. 970 (C.D. Ill. 1983), where a designer's performance specifications were allegedly so restrictive that they were deemed restrictive and discriminatory, aff'd. in part and remanded in part, Waldinger Corp. v. CRS Group Engineers, Inc. v. Clark Dietz Div., 775 F.2d 781 (7th Cir. 1985).

Walker v. Thornsberry, 97 Cal. App. 3d 842, 158 Cal. Rptr. 862 (1979).

Welch v. State of California, 139 Cal. App. 3d 546, 188 Cal. Rptr. 726 (1983).

Wm. R. Clarke Corp. v. Safeco Ins. Co., 15 Cal. 4th 882, 64 Cal. Rptr. 2d 578 (1997).

Worcester v. Granger Bros., Inc., 19 Mass. App. Ct. 379, 474 N.E.2d 1151, 1152 n.3, review denied, 394 Mass. 1103, 477 N.E.2d 595 (1985).

Index

C

D

L

M

N

O